T0149323

THE ROAD TO ENTREPRENEURSHIP

A Sure Way to Become Wealth at
INDIVIDUAL, BUSINESS AND STATE LEVELS.

KINGSTONE P. NGWIRA

authorHOUSE®

AuthorHouse™
1663 Liberty Drive
Bloomington, IN 47403
www.authorhouse.com
Phone: 1 (800) 839-8640

Published by AuthorHouse   03/11/2016

ISBN: 978-1-5049-8454-6 (sc)
ISBN: 978-1-5049-8452-2 (hc)
ISBN: 978-1-5049-8453-9 (e)

Library of Congress Control Number: 2016903918

Print information available on the last page.

Any people depicted in stock imagery provided by Thinkstock are models, and such images are being used for illustrative purposes only.
Certain stock imagery © *Thinkstock.*

This book is printed on acid-free paper.

Contents

Part IV
Creation of Wealth Through Entrepreneurship

PART V
Managing Within the Dynamic and Complex
Environment: Taking Risks and Making Profits

Part VI
The Legal Environment of Business

Acknowledgements

My thanks go to wonderful people who have worked so hard to make this edition a possibility. Dr. Joseph Shevel and Dr. Ndione Chauluka you have both been very helpful. Included as recipients of special thanks are Professor Kuthemba Mwale and Professor Brown Chimphamba for editorial consulting and Dr. David Kamchacha for editing assistance.

And last, but by no means least, I would like to thank all staff at Corporate Printing and Packaging Limited, Kingdom Publishing Company, Pentecostal Life University, Exploits University, Pentecostal Life FM and TV for their untiring efforts. The support to make this edition a success is acknowledged with gratitude.

PREFACE

IF YOU DEDICATE YOURSELF to applying the strategies presented in this book you will become wealthy and if you make this book part of your life it will make you rich. I can make those statements with complete confidence because the book has proven and tested principles. I deliver practical, proven instructions and it is believed that anyone that cares to apply himself or herself to the instructions presented in this nook is sure by heading for wealth. Other individual organizations try to sell hope alone, without the proven expertise to back it up, and just when you begin to realize that the advice you paid for is unproven and ineffective—they try to sell you more expensive products. They hook you on promises and never deliver. How will this book make you wealthy? That's a fair question, so let me give you a road map. Early in my career, it became obvious to me that education gives you a big edge in business. When you learn everything you can about what you're getting into, risk—which is always a part of doing business—is substantially reduced. People who are more educated—by that I mean savvy and prepared not just formally educated—have the advantage. That's what has made me so successful. The field of entrepreneurship is experiencing incredible rates of growth, not only in developing countries but across the world as well. People of all backgrounds, ages and stations of life are launching businesses of their own and in the process are reshaping the global economy through entrepreneurship at individual, business and state levels. Entrepreneurs willing to assume the risks of the market to gain its rewards are the heart of capitalism. These men and women with their bold entrepreneurial spirits will lead nations into wealth and prosperity throughout history.

Since an economy is composed of individuals, businesses (firms) and state levels, entrepreneurship embraced at these levels is significant force throughout nations. In every case, it is the entrepreneurs creating businesses that lead to nations out of jungles of economic oppression to higher standards of living and hope for the future.

It is time economies all over the world should move from free market economies (where only the individuals and firms are players) to mixed economies (where all three: individuals, firms and the state are players).

The purpose of this book is exciting each of the three levels that form the economy to look at the role of entrepreneurship as significant in wealth creation. Thus why entrepreneurs should be perceived as angels of economic growth and this book brings to them the material they need to launch and manage businesses successfully in the hotly competitive environment of the twenty - first century.

Similarly, the state whose function is to finance the public sector through taxation will need a vibrant private sector spearheaded by entrepreneurship to attain its required growth levels. I want this book to help all the three levels of an economy to become wealthy and specifically the entrepreneurs so that they write their own success story. Here's a tip for getting the most out of this book. Don't get overwhelmed by all the good ideas and the details. Focus on how you can implement these steps in the next 180 days. If you do, I guarantee it will put you on the path to prosperity, just like the subtitle says. Most people never take the time to come up with even a basic plan for building wealth and becoming financially secure—so by learning from an expert in this book, you are way ahead of the game. So read about it, but more importantly go and do it!

Kingstone P. Ngwira

INTRODUCTION

THANK YOU FOR MAKING a decision to read this book. In the pages ahead you are going to learn how entrepreneurship can create wealth at individual, business and state levels. When the principles and concepts presented in this book are practiced the economy of that nation will enjoy wealth. Many economists say that economy is composed of individuals (Households), firms and the state. The individuals and the firms form the micro – economics and the private sector while the state forms the macro-economics and the public sector. Series of practical and proven methods that work for wealth creation through entrepreneurship at these three levels have been presented. While most entrepreneurs start by forming small businesses not all businesses are entrepreneurial. Typically entrepreneurs are more focused on assembling resources and creating new innovative products and services that lead to investment and growth of an economy.

Every state has programmes to assist entrepreneurs and businesses yet the needs of entrepreneurs quickly diverge as a result of rapid entrepreneurial growth. Many states all over the world now begin to understand the unique role entrepreneurship plays in an economy that can contribute to wealth creation. States that wish to generate and improve wealth in an economy should develop deliberate policies that should nurture entrepreneurship at individual, business and state levels. Therefore it goes without saying that state policies that affect entrepreneurship in an economy should often be scattered throughout state government and do not fall completely within the purview of economic development. State policy makers should ask these questions as they consider policies to promote entrepreneurship within their economies:

- What role can entrepreneurship play in the state's current economy?

In answering these questions and in pursuit to wealth creation at individual, business and state levels the state as a major key player or actor should focus on these key policy areas:

- What will entrepreneurs need to be successful contributors to a healthy state economy?
- What specific programmes or policies address those needs?
- Access to capital and financing mechanisms
- Securities regulations
- Promotion of state programmes to entrepreneurs
- Recognition of entrepreneurial contributors to the state economy
- Building regulatory infrastructure
- Business registration and licensing
- Tax policy and compliance and
- Entrepreneurial education

The road to entrepreneurship is the bedrock of wealth creation at the aforementioned three levels of an economy. The dynamic nature of entrepreneurship may never be well enough identified to create comprehensive state economic development programmes that encompass all the areas important to entrepreneurial growth that will create wealth at the three levels. By facilitating this dynamic environment, the state can position itself to be attractive, competitive and resourceful public sector player in the economy.

PART I

Understanding Entrepreneurship

CHAPTER 1

Entrepreneurs: The Angels of Economic Growth

What is entrepreneurship?

MANY BUSINESS COMMENTATORS SAY THAT AN ENTREPRENEUR IS ONE who creates a new business in the face of risk and uncertainty for the purpose of achieving profit and growth by identifying opportunities and assembling the necessary resources to capitalize on those opportunities. Entrepreneurs usually start with nothing more than an idea – often a simple one – and then organize the resources necessary to transform that idea into a sustain-able business. Additionally, one business writer says an entrepreneur is "someone who takes nothing for granted, assumes change is possible and follows through someone incapable of confronting reality without thinking about ways to improve it and for whom action is a natural consequence of thought.

Many people dream of owning their businesses and become wealthy but most of them never launch the business or company. It goes without saying that those who take an entrepreneurial plunge will experience the thrill of creating some-thing grand from nothing; they will also discover the challenges and difficulties of building a business "from scratch". Whatever their reasons for choosing entrepreneurship many think that true satisfaction comes only from running their own businesses the way they choose.

Various studies have shown that researchers have invested a great deal of time and effort over the last decade studying these entrepreneurs and trying to paint a clear picture of the "entrepreneurial personality."

Although studies have produced several characteristics entrepreneurs tend to exhibit, none of them has isolated a set of traits required for success. The brief summary of entrepreneurial profile includes but not limited to: desire for responsibility, preference for moderate risk, confidence in their ability to succeed, desire for immediate feedback, high level of energy, future orientation, skill at organizing, value of achievement over money, high degree of commitment, tolerance of ambiguity, flexibility and tenacity.

The Entrepreneur

Many business gurus say that entrepreneurs have many of the same character traits as leaders. Similarly to the early great man theories of leadership; however trait based theories of entrepreneurship are increasingly being called into question. For example entrepreneurs are often constructed with managers and administrators who said to be more methodical and less prone to risk- talking. Such person centric models of entrepreneurship have shown questionable validity not least as many real life entrepreneurs operate in teams rather than as single individuals. Still, a vast but now clearly dated literature studying the entrepreneurial personality found that certain traits seem to be associated with entrepreneurs.

Real life situation has shown that there are four types of entrepreneurs: innovators, the calculating inventor, the over optimistic promoter, and the organization builder. These types are not related to the personality but to the type of opportunity the entrepreneur faces. Robinson (2010) mentions that for the entrepreneur to succeed he or she needs to process the following charactering: the entrepreneur should have an enthusiastic vision, the driving force of an enterprise; the entrepreneur's vision is usually supported by an interlocked collection of specific ideas not available to the market place; the overall blue print to realize the vision is clear, however details may be incomplete, flexible and involving, entrepreneur promotes the vision with enthusiastic passion; with persistence and de-termination, the entrepreneur develops strategies to change the vision into reality; the entrepreneur takes the initial responsibility to cause a vision to become a success; entrepreneurs take prudent risks. They asses cost, market / customer needs and persuade others to join and help; and an entrepreneur is usually a positive thinker and decision maker.

Development of Entrepreneurship

The understanding of entrepreneurship owes much to work of economist Joseph Schumpeter and the Austrian economists such as Ludwig von Mises and von Hayek. Schumpeter (1961) states that an entrepreneur is a person who is willing and able to convert a new idea or invention into successful innovations.

Entrepreneurship forces "creative destruction" in what's creative destruction is largely responsible for the dynamism of industries and long-run economic growth. Despite Schumpeter's early 20th century contributions, the traditional microeconomic growth of economies has had little room of entrepreneurs in its theoretical frameworks. Much of the literature on entrepreneurship can be di-vided into broad camps focus on individuals and structure respectively (peters 1998). They first seek to explain the prevalence of entrepreneurs in terms of innate psychological traits or how special characteristics are formed in certain social - cultural groups. The second highlights how social cultural structures call fourth entrepreneurs by providing opportunities for entrepreneurship. The goal is not always to explain entrepreneurial action on micro level, but rather the amount of entrepreneurial activity in a certain place or time (Radebaugh 2005).

An early and important contribution to the study of entrepreneurial individuals was David McClelland's the Achievement society '(1961). McClelland argued that some societies have cultural attitudes, which translate into primary socialization practices that foster entrepreneurial individuals. Nickels et al (2005) similarly argued that the entrepreneurial personality was the result of a particularly painful upbringing. Other researchers have sought the entrepreneurial personality in risk-taking propensity, internal locus of control, tolerance for ambiguity: over-optimism and need for autonomy (Stevenson 2005).

The structural traditional on the other hand seeks to understand how social, cultural and institution factors induce entrepreneurship. Some argued that deviance and marginality encourage entrepreneurship and marginality encourage entrepreneurship instead they emphasize that cultural and institutional support, including good access to resources, it is what encourages entrepreneurship (Sullivan 2001). Nickels et al (2005) break this down regulatory factors such as institutions and policies and cognitive factors such as knowledge on how to start ventures and obtain financial support and normative factors The perception of entrepreneurship as career which are used to explain both types and levels of entrepreneurship in different countries. Management researchers often emphasize the special influence of organizations and especially prior employment in established firms (Hisrich 1998).

Organizations are said to serve three critical functions: they provide opportunities to build confidence especially in the ability to create a new organization; provide general industry knowledge and specific formation about entrepreneurial opportunities; and provide social networks and access to critical resources (Daniel 2007).

As mentioned elsewhere these approaches typically seek to explain the amount of entrepreneurial activity. Both traditional have also been criticized for failing to account for entrepreneurial action on the micro level: the individuals approach for its single-cause logic, insensitivity to temporal dynamics and failure to ac-count for contextual factors, and the situational approach for its focus on adaptation and consequently failure to account for human agency. The current trend instead is to regard heterogeneity in terms of knowledge, preferences, abilities and behaviours as a fundamental assumption for theory building (Nickels at al 2005). The increased focus on heterogeneity naturally downplays interest in stable personality traits and broad contextual pressures in favour of more detailed investigations and explanations of entrepreneurial action.

Entrepreneurship in the 21ˢᵗ Century

This is an entrepreneurial age. Entrepreneurship is often perceived as a difficult undertaking, as a vast majority of new business fail. Entrepreneurial activities are substantially different depending on the type of organization that is being started. Entrepreneurship ranges in scale from solo projects also known as swivivalsts (individualism) to major undertaking many job opportunities.

Entrepreneurship is the sense of free enterprise because the birth of new business gives a market economy its vitality. Many business commentators say that the one extreme of an entrepreneur is a person of every high aptitude who pioneers change, processing characteristics found in only a very small fraction of the population. On the other hand, extreme definitions of anyone who wants to work for himself is considered to be an entrepreneur.

Peters (2012) supports the above views and states that entrepreneurship results in creation, enhancement, realization of value, not just for owners, for all participants and stakeholders. At the heart of this process is the creation and or recognition of opportunities followed by the will and initiative to seize these opportunities. Thus it requires willingness to take risks, both personal and financial- but in a very calculated fashion in order to constantly shift the odds to your favorable balancing the risks with potential reward.

Many writers share the above views and comment that entrepreneurs devise ingenious strategies to marshal their limited resources. This means that they are people who see opportunities where others see chaos. They move into an area and start making money while others wonder-what are these people doing on this dead place.

Economic prospective entrepreneurial on action

Schumpeter is arguably the most influential economist of entrepreneurship. In Schumpeter's writing the individual entrepreneur who embodies the innovation function in society and stands out as a leader in an entrepreneurship and embodies the innovation function in society and stands out as a leader in an otherwise equilibrating world of habitant actors. Contrary to the rest of the population, entrepreneurs are creative actors who are defined by their non-rational extraordinary qualities. Schumpeter saw information as having any unique knowledge or capabilities compared to non- entrepreneurs. Schumpeter rather emphasized the non-utilitarian qualities of entrepreneurs speculated about their unique psycho-logical makeup-up. Schumpeter also stressed the practical side of entrepreneur-ship, arguing that entrepreneurs are individuals that 'get things done' in so

CHAPTER 2

Business Opportunities

OFTEN THE MOST ATTRACTIVE opportunity for many people is that of owning and managing their own businesses. Millions of people all over the world have taken an entrepreneurial challenge and succeeded. Tremendous opportunities exist for all men and women willing to take the risk of starting a business. Before we look at different opportunities that are available let me de-fine what a business opportunity is. A business opportunity is finding a window that is open to access a customer who will bring revenue in exchange of the product or service which a seller has for sale. This means that when the window of opportunities closes the business will die. Presented below are business opportunities that are advocated by many writers and business commentators.

Start Up Business Opportunity

Starting a successful business requires preparation, special talents, skills, competencies and abilities, leadership skills as well as resources. These are critical requirements before you step into any business. Experience and observation has shown that many businesses both great and small fail because of poor or lack of preparation. You need to know that Prior Proper Preparation Prevents Poor Performance.

So I would like to say congratulations! The decision to start your own business can be one of the best you will ever make in your life. Owning your own business should be an exhilarating, inspiring, grand adventure; one full of new sights and experiences, delicious highs and occasional lows, tricky paths and, hopefully, big open sky's. But to ensure that your business journey will be a fruitful one, it is important to understand all that an entrepreneur entails.

Setting up new business collides with the wishes of established competitors, who want all the customers' income they can get. Many people start their business adventure dreaming of riches and freedom. And while both are certainly possible, the first thing to understand is that there are trade-offs when you decide to start a business. Difficult bosses, annoying co-workers, peculiar policies, demands upon your time, and limits on how much money you can make are traded for independence, creativity, opportunity, and power. But by the same token, you also swap a regular pay check and benefits for no pay check and no benefits. A life of security, comfort, and regularity is traded for one of uncertainty.

Start – up influences

Why does anybody want to take the risk of starting up their own business? It is hard work without guaranteed results. But millions do so every year around the world. The start-up is the bedrock of modern – day commercial wealth, the foundation of free-market economics upon which competition is based. So can economists shade light on the process?

Economists would tell us that new entrants into an industry can be expected when there is a rise in expected post-entry profitability for them. In other words, new entrants expect to make extra profits. Economists tell us that the rate of en-try is related to the growth of the industry. They also tell us the entry is deterred by barriers such as high capital requirements, the existence of economies of scale, product differentiation and restricted access to necessary in puts and so on. What is more the rate of entry is lower in industries with high degrees of concentration where it may be assumed that firms combine to deter entry. However, research also tells us that whereas the rate of small firm start-up in these concentrated industries is lower, the rate of start-up for large firms is higher.

These seem useful, but perhaps obvious statements about start-ups, really hap-pen and why? Somehow economists fail to explain convincingly the rationale for, and the process of, start-up. They seem to assume that there is a continuous flow of entrants into an industry just waiting for the possibility of extra profits. But people are not like that. They need to earn money to live; they have families who depend on them.

Benefits of Owning Your Own Business or Company

Surveys show that owners of businesses or companies believe they work harder, earn more money and are happier than if they worked for someone or for a corporation. Before launching any business venture every potential entrepreneur should consider the benefits and opportunities of business ownership. The following are benefits of owning your own business: You gain control over your own destiny, you have opportunity to make a difference, reap unlimited returns, contribute to society and be recognised for your efforts. More importantly you also have an opportunity to do what you love doing and reach full potential.

- ### *Buying an Existing Business*

For many entrepreneurs the quickest way to enter a market is to purchase an existing business. Yet, the attraction of fast entry can be a great mistake. Buying an existing business requires a great deal of analysis and evaluation to ensure that what you are really purchasing is really meeting your needs. So you do not need to rush. For starters be sure that you have considered answers to the following questions:

1. Is this the type of business you would like to operate?
2. Do you know the negative aspects of this type of business?
3. Is this the best market for this business?
4. Do you know the critical factors for this business to be successful?
5. Do you have experience required to run this type of business?
6. Will you need to make any changes to the business?
7. If the business is currently in a decline do you have what it takes to make it profitable?
8. If the business is profitable why is the current owner want to sell it?
9. Have you examined other businesses that are currently for sale?

Many of these questions ask you to be honest with yourself about your ability to operate the business successfully. On one hand buying an existing business has the following advantages: an established successful business may continue to be successful; the new owner can use the experience of the previous owner; the new owner hits the ground running; an existing business may already have the best location; employees and suppliers are already in place; equipment is installed and productive capacity is known and finding financing is easier. On the other hand buying an existing business has the following disadvantages: It's a loser. A business may be for sale because it has never been profitable; the previous owner may have created ill will; current employees may not be suitable; the business location may become unnecessary; equipment and facilities may be obsolete; change and innovation may be difficult to implement; accounts receivable may be less than the face value and sometimes the business may be overpriced.

The Potential Drawbacks of Entrepreneurship

Although owning a business has many benefits and provides many opportunities anyone planning to enter the world of entrepreneurship should be aware of potential drawbacks.

• *Uncertainty of Income*

Opening and running a business provides no guarantees that an entrepreneur will earn enough money to survive. Some businesses barely earn enough to provide the owner manager with an adequate income. In the early days of the business entrepreneurs often have trouble meeting financial obligations and may have to live on savings. The regularity of income that comes with working for someone is absent.

• *Risk of Losing Your Entire Invested Capital*

The startup business failure rate often very high. Many studies have shown that 34 percent of new businesses fail within two years and 50 percent shut down within four years. Within six years, 60 percent of new businesses will have folded.

• *Long Hours and Hard Work*

Business start ups often demand that owners keep nightmarish schedules. In many start – ups, 10 to 12 hour days and 6 or 7 day work – weeks with no paid vacations are the norm. Because they often must do everything themselves, own-ers experience intense, draining workdays.

• *Lower Quality of Life Until Business Gets Established*

The long hours and hard work needed to launch a company can take their toll on the remainder of an entrepreneurs life. Business owners often find that their roles as husband and wives or fathers and mothers take a back seat to their roles as company founders.

• *High Levels of Stress*

Launching and running a business can be extremely rewarding experience, but it also can be a highly stressful one. Most entrepreneurs have made significant investments in their companies, have left behind the safety and security of a steady pay check and mortgaged everything they owned to get into business. Failure means total financial ruin as well as a serious psychological blow and that creates high levels of stress and anxiety.

• *Discouragement*

Launching a business requires much dedication, discipline and tenacity. Along the way to building a successful business, entrepreneurs will run headlong into many obstacles, some of which may appear to be insurmountable. Discouragement and disillusionment can set in but successful entrepreneurs know that every business encounters rough spots and that perseverance is required to get through them.

The Ten Deadly Mistakes of Entrepreneurship

Going into business of whatever nature requires seriousness. Studies as well as many business commentators say that because of limited resources, inexperienced management and lack of financial stability, many business ventures suffer a mortality rate significantly higher than that of larger established businesses. Exploring the causes of business failure may help you avoid them. Let us now look at the ten deadly mistakes of entrepreneurship advocated by various business gurus.

• Lack of Experience

An entrepreneur needs to have experience in the field he or she wants to enter. For example, if a person wants to open a retail clothing business, he should first work in a retail clothing store. This will give him practical experience as well as help him learn the nature of business. This type of experience can spell the difference between failure and success.

Ideally, a prospective entrepreneur should have adequate technical ability; a working knowledge of the physical operations of the business; sufficient conceptual ability; the power to visualize, coordinate and integrate the various operations of the business into a synergistic whole and skill to manage people in the organization and motivate them to higher levels of performance.

• Management Incompetence

In most business ventures management inexperience or poor decision making ability is the chief problem of the failing enterprise. The owner lacks leadership ability and knowledge necessary to make the business work.

• Undercapitalization

Sound management is the key to entrepreneurial success and effective managers realize that any successful business venture requires proper financial control. The margin for error in managing finances is especially small for most entrepreneurs and neglecting to install proper financial controls is recipe for disaster. Two pitfalls affecting entrepreneurs' business financial health are common: undercapitalization and poor cash management.

Many entrepreneurs make the mistake of beginning their businesses on a "shoestring" which is a fatal error leading to business failure. Entrepreneurs tend to be overly optimistic and often underestimate the financial requirements of launching a business or the amount of time required for the business or company to become self – sustaining. As a result they start off undercapitalized and can never seem to catch up financially as their companies consume increasing amounts of cash to fuel growth.

• *Poor Cash Management*

Insufficient Cash Flow due to poor cash management is a common cause of business failure. Companies need adequate cash flow to thrive, without it a company is out of business. Maintaining adequate cash flow and to pay bills in a timely fashion is a constant challenge for most entrepreneurs especially those in a start – up phase or more established companies experiencing growth. Fast – growing companies devour cash fast! Poor credit and collection practices on accounts receivables, sloppy accounts payable practices that exert undue pres-sure on a company's cash balance and uncontrolled spending are common to many business ventures bankruptcies.

• *Lack of Strategic Management*

Too many entrepreneurs neglect the process of strategic management because they think that it is something that only benefits large companies. "I don't have the time" or "We are too small to develop a strategic plan," they often rationalize. Failure to plan usually results in failure to survive. Without a clear defined strategy a business has no sustainable basis for creating and maintaining a competitive edge in the market place.

• *Weak Market Effort*

Business success requires a sustained, creative marketing effort to draw a base of customers and to keep them coming back. Creative entrepreneurs find ways to market their businesses effectively to their target customers without breaking the bank.

• *Uncontrolled Growth*

Growth is a natural, healthy and desirable part of any business enterprise but it must be planned and controlled. Peter Drucker says that start – up companies can expect to outgrow their capital bases each time sales increase 40 to 50 per-cent. Ideally entrepreneurs finance the expansion of their companies by the profits they generate ("retained earnings") or by capital contributions from the owners, but most businesses wind up borrowing at least a portion of the capital in-vestment.

• *Poor Location*

For any business choosing the right location is partly an art and partly a science. Too often entrepreneurs select their locations without adequate research and investigation. Some beginning owners choose a particular location just because they noticed a vacant building. But the location principle is too critical to leave to chance. There is also need to consider the rate of rent. Location has two important features: what it costs and what it generates in the sales volume.

• *Inability to Make the "Entrepreneurial Transition"*

If a business fails, it is most likely to do so in its first five years of life. Making it over the "entrepreneurial start up hump," however, is no guarantee of business success. After the start up, growth usually requires a radically different style of leadership and management. Many businesses fail when their founders are un-able to make the transition from entrepreneur to manager and are unwilling to bring professional management. The very abilities that make an entrepreneur successful often lead to managerial ineffectiveness. Growth requires entrepreneurs to delegate authority and to relinquish hands – on control to daily operations, something many entrepreneurs simply can't do. Their business's success requires that they avoid micromanaging and become preservers and promoters of their companies' vision, mission, core values and culture.

• *Putting Failure into Perspective*

Because entrepreneurs are building businesses in an environment filled with uncertainty and shaped by rapid change, entrepreneurs recognize that failure is likely to be part of their lives and they are not paralyzed by that fear. "The excitement of building a new business from scratch is far greater than the fear of failure." Says, one entrepreneur who failed several times before finally succeeding. Successful entrepreneurs have the attitude that failures are simply stepping stones along the path of success. This leads to a conclusion that failure is a natural part of the creative process. The only people who never fail are those who never do anything or never attempt anything new. One hall mark of successful entrepreneurs is the ability to fail intelligently, learning why they failed so that they can avoid making the same mistake again.

They know that business success does not depend on their ability to avoid making mistakes but to be open to the lessons each mistake brings. They learn from their failures and use them as fuel to push themselves closer to their ultimate target. Entrepreneurs are less worried about what they might lose if they try something and fail than about what they miss if they fail to try. The entrepreneurial success requires both persistence and resilience, the ability to bounce back from failures.

How to Avoid the Pitfalls

As valuable as failure can be to the entrepreneurial process, no one sets out to fail. We have seen some of the most common reasons behind business failures. Now we must examine the ways to avoid becoming another failure statistic and gain insight into what makes a start up successful. Entrepreneurial success re-quires much more than just a good idea for a product or service. It also takes solid plan execution, adequate resources such as capital and people, the ability to assemble and manage those resources and perseverance. Strategies to avoid the pitfalls include: knowing your business in depth; preparing a good business plan; managing financial resources well; understanding financial statements; managing people effectively; having a competitive advantage over rivals; leveraging (doing more with the less) and financial intelligence.

CHAPTER 3

Financing the Business

Decide on Business Finance: Equity or Debt

IN FINANCIAL REPORTING, we normally deal with financial statements that an organization's accounting system produces including the profit and loss account also commonly called Income Statement, the balance sheet and cash flow statements. The income statement presents the financial performance, the statement of financial position also called balance sheet presents the financial position while cash flow represents the financial adaptability. Out of the three financial statements the balance sheet which represents assets, capital and liabilities shows how the business is financed.

Show me the Money

Finding the funds to start your business is usually one of the most challenging things the budding entrepreneur will face. Whether yours is a small, home-based business or a large venture that requires six-or seven-figure funding, the good news is that money is available. The bad news is that it is sometimes harder to secure than you may anticipate. But look around. Every one of those businesses that you see as you drive down the street began as someone's dream and, some-how, those entrepreneurs found the money to open their doors. If they did, so can you.

New businesses normally have difficult time securing money for a variety of reasons. Conventional financing may be difficult because a new business is a risk to banks—there is no track record or assets to go on. For this reason, almost 75 percent of all start-up businesses are funded through other means. In this chapter, those other options are examined.

Money and the New Business

The very first thing required of you is to accurately estimate the amount of money you need. Taking a cold, hard look at your money requirements will help you know your business better and help ensure your success. Once you know how much capital your business will require, it will be incumbent on you to get it. Having a cash crunch from the start is a sure way to go out of business fast. Moreover, a realistic budget will help convince a lender or investor that you understand your business and are worth the risk. The first thing any investor will want to know is how much money you will need and how you plan to spend it. They will want specific details on how the money will be spent and how you plan to repay the money.

How much money do you need?

If you have created a business plan, you should have a pretty good idea how much money you will need to get started. If you have not figured it out yet, this section will help you. The money you will need can be divided into three categories: one-time costs, working capital, and ongoing costs. One-time costs are things that you will need to spend money on to start your business but will unlikely see again, such as: Legal and ac-counting costs. You may need to hire a lawyer to help you negotiate contracts, incorporate, or perform other legal services. An accountant may be needed to set up your books. Working capital is the money you will need to keep your business going until you start to make a profit. The old adage "it takes money to make money" is true and real. It is critical to have enough working capital on hand to cover the following costs: Debt payments. If you will be borrowing money to get started, you will want to begin repaying it right away. Service businesses have little, if any inventory, but retail and wholesale companies often spend large sums in this area.

Business finance therefore deals with deciding the capital structure. Capital structure explains how the business is financed. Businesses are financed either by equity capital or debt capital. These are the main sources of finance. How-ever, each of these has cost of acquisitioning the funds. Thus if funds are acquired from equity holders the business will pay cost of equity to its shareholders and if funds have been acquired from lenders of finance such as banks the business pays cost of debt normally this is an interest.

Although debt is a way of financing a business in many cases the financial institutions such as banks do not provide the funds to a newly established business because normally banks look for financial statement or collateral of which the business might not have because it is just starting. So this leaves only one option of financing the business that is just starting with equity funds.

Since they are two options for financing the business: equity or debt you can also decide to obtain the funds from both equity holders (your own funds) and the banks at the same time. Therefore in most cases, a company's funds may be viewed as a pool of resource, that is, a combination of different funds with different costs. Under such circumstances it might seem appropriate to use an average cost of capital for investment approval.

Weighted average cost of capital is the average cost of company's finance (equity, debentures, bank loans etc) weighted according to the proportion each element bears to the total pool of capital. Weighting is usually based on market valuations, current yields and cost after tax. However, the question is that higher level of borrowing increases the financial risk and this must be avoided.

CHAPTER 4

Location and Facilities Layout

LOCATING A BUSINESS IN the right place is important because the cost of moving output and people across space is significant. For example, the best site for a retail store generally is one that is in close proximity to a large number of people who are the potential customers of the store. In contrast a manufacturing firm may combine raw materials from several sources and ship manufactured output to customers at other sites. In this case, an important criterion for location is the cost of shipping raw material relative to the cost of shipping final output. Another consideration is that all firms employ workers who must travel from their homes to the firm each working day.

An entrepreneur's ultimate goal is to locate the business at a site that will maximize the likelihood of success. The more entrepreneurs invest in researching potential locations the higher is the probability that they will find the spot that is best suited for the company. The trick is to keep an open mind about where the location of the business might be.

Consideration in selecting the best location should consider the following questions: whether the business should be closer to the customer or closer the supplier (raw material source) or in the centre between the customer and supplier. Additionally, the cost of shipping the input and output should also be considered. Amongst location decisions the entrepreneur must also consider locating the firm in close proximity to that labour supply or face the prospect of paying premium wages to compensate workers for travelling long distances and/ or providing housing.

Location Factors in Real World Situation

Obviously, the process used by managers to select location for a plant is more involving than that suggested by the preceding theoretical discussion but the process is consistent with theory. In general, all significant factors that will influence the profitability are evaluated at each location under consideration. Be-cause both revenue and cost may differ at each location, the analysis must consider each location's attributes as they affect these two variables. The locational attributes described here are fundamental in the decision to locate an industrial facility. Although for particular firms some are more important than others, a significant shortfall in the ability to provide even one of these may greatly reduce the attractiveness of that site.

PART II

Venturegrowth

CHAPTER 5

Venture Growth Stages

WHEN THE BUSINESS IS BORN OR START IT IS EXPECTED TO GROW. FIGURE 6.1 BELOW PRESENTS THE traditional life- cycle stages of an enterprise. These stages include new venture development, start-up activities, growth, stabilization, and innovation or decline.

Figure 6.1: Venture Growth Stages

Profitability

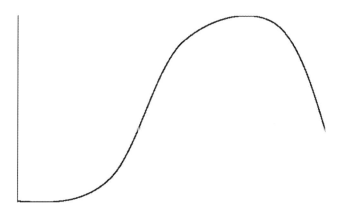

Revenue

New-Venture Venture Business Innovation Growth
Start – up Growth Stabilization or Decline

Source: Ngwira (2015), Development Activities

New Venture Development

The first stage, of new venture development, consists of activities associated with the initial formulation of the venture. This initial phase is the foundation of entrepreneurial process and requires creativity and assessment.

In addition to the accumulation and expansion of resources, this is a creativity, assessment, and networking stage for initial entrepreneurial strategy formulation. Thus the enterprise general philosophy, mission, scope and direction are deter-mined during this stage.

Start-up activities

The second stage, is start- up activities, which encompasses the foundation work for creating a formal business plan, searching for capital, carrying out market activities and developing an effective entrepreneurial team. These activities typically demand an aggressive entrepreneurial strategy with maximum efforts de-voted to launching the venture. This stage is similar to chandler's description of rationalization of the use of the firm's resources. Strategic and operational plan-ning steps designed to identify the firm's competitive advantage and operational planning steps designed to identify it. Many business managers say that marketing and financial considerations tend to be paramount during this stage.

Growth

The growth stage often requires major changes in entrepreneurial strategy. Com-petition and other marketing forces call for the reformation of strategies. For example some firms find themselves "growing out" of business because they are unable to cope with the growth of their ventures. Many business commentators say that highly creative entrepreneurs sometimes are unable, or unwilling, to meet the administrative challenges that accompany this growth stage. As a result they leave the ventures and move on to other ventures. The creative ideas are detrimental to the growth of the venture. The firm needed a managerial entrepreneur to run the operations: jobs had neither the expertise nor the desire to assume this role.

The growth stage presents newer and more substantial problems than those the entrepreneur faced during the start-up stage. These newer challenges force the entrepreneur into developing step of skills while maintaining an "entrepreneurial perspective" for the organization. Thus the growth stage is a transition from entrepreneurial one person leadership to managerial team-oriented leadership

Business Stabilization

Business commentators say that the stabilization stage is a result of both marketing conditions and the entrepreneur's efforts. During this stage a number of developments commonly occur, including increased competition, consumer difference to the entrepreneur's good(s) or service(s) and situation of the market with a host of "me too" looks-likes. Thus sales often begin to stabilize and entrepreneur begins thinking about the enterprise will go over the next three years. Many writers describe this stage as a swing stage in that it preceeds the period when the firm either swings into higher gear and greater profitability of swings toward decline and failure. During this stage innovations is often critical to future success.

Innovation or Decline

Generally firms that fail to innovate will die. Financially successful enterprises often will try to acquire other innovative firms, thereby ensuring their own growth. Also, many firms will work on new products/ services development in order to enhance current offerings.

Why so many businesses fail

According to longitudinal study conducted by Jones (2005), approximately 60% of small businesses shut down within the first six years. Such businesses fail to grow for numerous reasons. The most common reasons are: because their owners grow their company too fast: have a poor concept: are not good at marketing or sales: fail to plan: start their company without enough money to get to breakeven: have an inability to differentiate: lack control of their finances and books:

or don't build systems and processes. Many entrepreneurs who do not manage their finances and books: or don't build systems and processes. Many entrepreneurs who end up unsuccessful do not build processes and systems and lack the ability or desire to sell.

They do not carefully plan their business and often fail to raise the needed capital to sustain it until it is profitable. They do not focus on efficiency of operations or automation. They make the investment in additional capital or employees needed to expand the company to the point where it can make profit. As an entrepreneur, even if one has a great idea, one will have to plan well, build a long term team, make sure to have adequate capitalization, build the proper systems, and execute the plan.

Many business commentators say that there are certain critical success factors in building a successful small business. These include: vision of the management: passion: a good idea: clean, focused business objectives: a well thought through business plan: good organization: enthusiasm in the owners: a good team: motivated employees: good cash flow management: adequate financial resources: a clear understanding of marketing need: and execution of the management.

CHAPTER 6

Developing the Business Plan

ONE OF THE BUSINESS CONSULTANTS BY THE NAME BRIAN TRACY SAYS YOUR ABILITY TO PLAN AND ORGANIZE every detail of your great business is essential to your success and profitability. He further says a good business plan must contain values: clear, core principles Vision: ideal picture of the future of the business, mission: goals to accomplish, purpose: reasons why business exists, excellent leadership and management, excellent products and services, excellent reputation in market and solid financials. He continues to point out that crafting a good business plan requires thinking and the quality of your thinking about the key elements of your business has the greatest impact of all on your success and needs you to answer questions like what are the core values and principles that you and your business stand for and believe in? If your business was perfect in every way, what would it look like in future? What is your mission for your business defined in terms of how you would want to change or improve the life or work of your customers?

It goes without saying that solid business plans do not guarantee success. But for entrepreneurs with decent ideas, they surely boost the odds. A good plan accomplishes three important tasks.

Many business writers say that to have a winning business plan one has to start with a clear, concise executive summary of his business. Thus thinking of it like an elevator pitch. The following are also suggested by many business commentators: in no more than two pages, billboard all the important stuff. At the top, communicate your value proposition: what your company does, how it will make money and why customers will want to pay for your product or service. If you are sending your plan to investors, include the amount of money you need and how you plan to use it. You have to know the whole picture before you can boil things down, so tackle the summary after finishing the rest of your plan. Next, establish the market opportunity. Answer questions like: How large is your target market? How fast is it growing? Where are the opportunities and threats, and how will you deal with them? Again, highlight your value proposition. Most of this market information can be found through industry associations, chambers of commerce, census data or even from other business owners. (Be sure to source all of your information in case you are asked to back up your claims or need to update your business plan.)

CHAPTER 7

Competitive Advantage Issues

BOFEFORE WE GO INTO THE ROOTES COMPETITIVE ADVANTAGE IT IS IMPORTANT TO POINT OUT what distinguishes you from the competition in the minds of your customers. Whether you are an employee, a business or a country, you need to have a clear competitive advantage and communicate it to your customers. Before you can determine your competitive ad-vantage, you' need to know these three determinants:

Competitive advantage deals with areas of specialization. The entrepreneur should single out which area of specialization he is good at than his competitors. This could be in the area of skills, competencies, talents and abilities. If you do not have competitive advantage then do not compete. The competitive priorities discussed in chapter 13 such as quality, speed, dependability, flexibility and cost (doing business cheaply) should be considered. Additionally, there is also need to understand the nature of competition whether it is direct or indirect. Competitor analysis should be done to find out who are the real competitors, what are their strengths and weaknesses, what could be the advantages over them and what makes you unique than them?

Building a Competitive Advantage

The goal of developing a strategic plan is to create for the business a competitive advantage – the aggregation of factors that sets the business apart from its com-petitors and gives the unique position in the chosen market arena. From a strate-gic perspective the key to business success is to develop a unique competitive advantage, one that creates value for customers and is difficult for competitors to duplicate.

To be effective these competencies should be difficult for competitors to dupli-cate and they must provide customers with some kind of perceived benefit. As stated earlier company's core competencies often have to do with advantages of their size – agility, speed, closeness to their customers, superior service and ability to innovate. The key success is building these core competencies and concen-trating them on providing superior service and value for its target customers. However, it should be noted that developing core competencies does not neces-sarily require a company to spend a great deal of money. It does however require an entrepreneur to use creativity, imagination and vision to identify those things that it does best and that are most important to its target customers.

Building for a company's strategy around its core competencies allows the busi-ness to gain a sustainable competitive edge over its rivals and to ride its strategy to victory.

Porter's Five Forces: A model for Industry Analysis

Michael Porter argues that a business or a corporation is most concerned with the intensity of competition within industry. The level of this intensity is determined by basic competitive forces. He argues that the collective strengths of these forces determines the ultimate profit potential in the industry, where profit poten-tial is measured in terms of long-run return on invested capital. Michael Porter points out that the five forces presented below are what determines the industry competition.

Threat of New Entrant

New entrants to an industry typically bring to its new capacity, a desire to gain market share, and substantial resources. They are, therefore, threats to an established cooperation. The threat of entry depends on the presence of entry barriers and the reaction that can be expected from existing competitors. An entry barrier is an obstruction that makes it difficult for a company to enter an industry. Some of the possible barriers to entry are:

- Economies of scale. Economies of scale occur when a firm grows in size and experience reduction in costs as a result of increasing production.
- Product differentiation. These are the differences in the production or appearances of a product.
- Sometimes it can occur through high levels of advertising and promotion.
- Capital requirements. This occurs when an existing firm has huge financial resources to create a significant barrier to entry to any competitor.
- Switching costs. These are costs that a firm would incur,. e.g. training costs, if it were to switch to new programs.
- Government policy. Governments can limit entry into an industry through licensing requirements by restricting access to raw materials, such as off-shore oil drilling sites.
- Accessing to distribution channels. Small entrepreneurs often have difficulty obtaining supermarket shelf space for their goods because large retailers charge for space and on their shelves and give priority to established firms who can pay for the advertising needed to generate high customer demand.

Rivalry Amongst Existing Firms

In most industries, corporations are mutually dependent. A competitive move by one firm can be expected to have a noticeable effect on its competitors and thus may cause retaliation or counter-efforts. According to Porter, intense rivalry is related to the presence of several factors, including:

- Number of competitors. When competitors are few and roughly equal in size they watch each other carefully to make sure that any move by another firm is matched by an equal countermove.
- Rate of industry growth. For example, any showing in passenger traffic tends to set off price wars in the airline industry because the only path to grow is to take sales away from a competitor.
- Amount of fixed costs. For example, because airlines must fly their planes on a schedule regardless of the number of paying passengers for any one flight, they offer cheap standby fares whenever a plane has empty seats.

- Capacity. If the only way a manufacturer can increase capacity is in a large increment by building a new plant, it will run that new plant at full capacity to keep its unit costs as low as possible – thus producing so much that the selling price falls throughout the industry.
- Diversity of rivals. Rivals that have very different ideas of how to compete are likely to cross paths often and unknowingly challenge each other's position.

Threats of Substitute Products or Services

Substitute products are those products that appear to be different but can satisfy the same needs as another product. For instance, in Malawi, coffee is a substitute for tea. Substitutes limit the potential returns of an industry by placing a ceiling on the prices firms in the industry can profitably charge. If the price of coffee goes up high enough, coffee drinkers will slowly begin switching to tea. The price of tea thus puts a price ceiling on the price of coffee.

CHAPTER 8

Business Growth Strategies

FIRMS ARE OF LIMITED SIZE although there are concentrates on their rates of growth. The past size and nature of constraints limiting the rate at which it can grow from that size and the objectives of those running it help explain growth of the firm. Constraints of growth can be analysed from conceptual framework within the development of theory of growth of the firm, thereafter examination can be done. However, the growth of a business should be based on keeping costs both fixed and variable costs low and maintaining profit and sales maximization which has a direct contribution to growth of the value of a business.

Rate of Growth for Firms

Growth and decline are complimentary aspects of the competitive process the economy as a whole. The three broad categories of restraint have been isolated and these are: financial, demand and managerial. Market structures and conver-sion governing business behaviour – affect this dispersion of efficiency between firms and the rate of technical progress.

In order to expand capacity finance is required. Whether raised internally or ex-ternally, access to finance will depend on the rate of profit vis-à-vis ploughing back into the firm. Customers can be attracted by price reduction. Beyond a cer-tain point the further attraction of customers will be at the expense of the rate of profit.

Since the rate of capacity expansion varies directly with the rate of profit and the rate of profit varies inversely with the rate of customers expansion, there will be maximum sustainable rate of growth at the simultaneous determined price and rate of profit are such as to enable customers and capacity to grow at the same rate. The operation of the transfer mechanism itself brings into play a counter-force called the innovation mechanisms.

Production Opportunity Resources and Services

The firm is conceived as a pool of productive resources organized within an ad-ministrative framework. In order to explore the concept of the productive oppor-tunity a distinction between productive resources and productive services is in-troduced. The uniqueness of each individual firm is based on the fact that firm's managerial team will have acquired experience and skills in combining resources of the firm's particular historical development.

The Managerial Restraint

It goes without saying that growth does not come automatically, it has to be planned. The collective experience of managerial team will determine the char-acter and important extent of the productive services available for expansion. Time is needed to gain experience in managing the particular firm that the new comer has joined. Such experience can be acquired on the job by learning from working with the existing managerial team.

The Direction of Expansion

The question is what will determine the direction in which the firm will expand. The answer is found in external inducement and internal inducement that changes in demand, technological innovation (external induces). External and internal inducements deal with overcoming the changing environmental condi-tions, resources are never fully utilized, some yes, some no.

Financing Growth

In chapter 3 it is pointed out that businesses are financed either by equity or debt capital. Experience has shown that growth of businesses can be financed by eq-uity or debt finance. This means that use of retained profits, reserves, preference share capital, new share issues as well as borrowing from financial institutions are the best forms of financing growth.

However, the effect of a new issue of shares on the market value of a firm's ex-isting shares will depend upon the expected profitability of the expansion. The final source of funds are the industrious led positions. On the assumption that the current market value of the firm depends on future dividends and capital gains, there will be a tradeoff between dividends and returns.

Organic Growth

This occurs when a business grows by using its existing resources. Organic growth can take place because the market is growing, or because the business organization is doing increasingly better than its competitors or is entering new markets. Exploiting a product advantage can sustain organic growth. Organic growth depends on a firm's available resources and capabilities as well as its planning, time and cash.

Mergers and Acquisitions

One of the fastest routes to growth is through an acquisition or merger, but it is one of the hardest and riskiest. There are two views about mergers. One is that mergers between titans will result in an even larger titan, too cumbersome to op-erate as flexibly and efficiently as it needs to. According to this view a merger results in more bureaucracy, diminishing returns negating the benefits of increases in size and capacity for production, diseconomies of scale, swallowing huge quantities of capital and causing organizational lethargy; and a lumbering giant that will be outpaced and outsmarted by smaller rivals. The second, more optimistic, view is that mergers result in: economies of scale and efficiency; sta-bility and greater potential for growth resulting from a broader base of customers and products; and an intellectual capital and management infrastructure to deal with market change.

Specialization

The opposite of diversification is specialization which involves dropping non-core activities, or even redefining and focusing on core operations. The main advantages are clear focus and strength in depth, with all available resources channeled into one endeavour. It also means that any cash available from the sale of non-core operations can be used to grow on the business. Re-iance on specialization requires doing what you do sufficiently better than your competi-tors and successfully anticipating and adapting to market changes.

Competitive Advantage

When a firm sustains profit that exceeds the average of its industry, the firm is said to possess a competitive advantage over its rivals. The goal of much of business strategy is to achieve a sustainable competitive advantage. Michael Porter identified two basic types of competitive advantage: cost advantage and differentiation. A competitive advantage exists when the firm is able to deliver the same benefits as competitors but at lowest cost (cost advantage), or deliver benefits that exceed those of competing products (differentiation advantage). Thus a competitive advantage enables the firm to create superior value for its customers and superior profits for itself.

Cost and differentiation advantages are known as position advantages since they describe the firm's position in the industry as a leader in either cost or differentiation. A resource based view emphasizes that a firm utilizes its resources and capabilities to create a competitive advantage that ultimately results in superior value creation.

Segmentation Strategy

What is market segmentation? Is a relatively homogeneous group of customers who will respond to a marketing mix in a similar way. Market segmentation is a two way process: naming broad product markets and segmenting those broad markets in order to select target markets and develop suitable marketing mixes.

A good market segmentation should have the following characteristics: homoge-neous (similar) customers in a segment should be as similar as possible with respect to their behaviour and likely responses, heterogeneous (different) cus-tomers in different segments should be as different as possible with respect to their likely responses, substantial - the segment should be big enough to be prof-itable, operational - the seg-menting dimensions should be useful for identifying customers and deciding on marketing mix variables. Reasons for segmentation include:

to understand the customers, to focus activities, to reduce risks, to defeat the competitors and to assist in planning.

There are three ways to develop market oriented strategies in a broad product market. The single target market approach - segmenting the market and picking one of the homogeneous segments as the firm's target market, the multiple target ap-proach -segmenting the market and choosing two or more seg-ments then treating each as a separate target market needing a different marketing mix and the combined target market ap-proach - combining two or more submarkets into one larger market as a basis for one strategy. All these three approaches involve target marketing. (1) and (2) are called segmenters and (3) are called combiners. They try to increase the size of their target market by combining two or more segments. Segmenters aim at one or more homogeneous segments. They try to develop a different marketing mix for each segment. Segmenters usually adjust their market mixes for each target market. Segmenters believe that aiming at one or some of these smaller markets makes it possible to satisfy the tar-get customers better and provide greater profit potential for the firm. These include geo-graphical, behavioural and demographic characteristics, qualifying dimensions are those relevant to including a customer type in a product market.

While determin-ing dimensions include those that actually affect the customer's purchase of a specific product or brand in a product market. Cluster analysis and positioning are a more sophisticated computer aided techniques of segmenting the market. It involves finding similar patterns within sets of data. Focusing on target markets helps one to fine tune the marketing mix.

Positioning

This is another approach which helps identify product market opportunities. Posi-tioning shows how customers locate pro-posed or present brands in market. It entails some formal marketing research. Managers should decide whether to leave the product (and marketing mix) alone or reposition it f an advert. This may mean physical changes in the product or simply image changes based on promotion. Firms often use promotion to help "position" how a product meets a target market's specific needs. Positioning helps managers understand how custom-ers see their market. This is called "perceptual mapping".

BCG Growth – Share Matrix

Businesses that are big enough to be organized into strategic business units face the challenge of allocating resources among those units. Boston Consulting Group (BCG) developed a mod-el for managing a portfolio of different business units (or major product lines).

Experience Curve Fig 10:1 Experience Curve

Cost

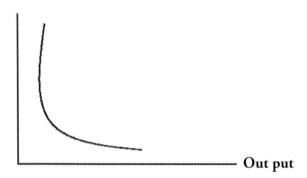

Source: Ngwira (2015)

The premises of the BCG findings are these: That in any market segment of an industry price level tends to be very sim-ilar for products. Therefore what makes one company more profitable than the rest must be the levels of its costs. It is the key determinants of low cost levels that the BCG attempted to unearth. Their arguments can be summarised as follows:

Total Units Produced

The relationship between unit costs and total costs produced over time. Signifi-cant cost is a function of experience and then cost is a function of a market share. Market share does not necessarily relate to the overall market. The overall implications of BCG's findings are that successful companies make almost all their profits from products in which they dominate their mar-ket segment. This view has become a very strong influence on many company's choices of strategy

Product Portfolio

In order to dominate a market a company must normally gain that dominance when the market is in growth stage of the product life cycle. In a state of maturity a market is likely to be stable with customer loyalties fairly fixed. It is therefore more difficult to gain share. The BCG has suggested the model of the product portfolio or the growth share matrix as a tool by which to consider product strat-egy. The matrix combines mar-ket growth rate and market share and thus directly relates to the idea of the experience curve

The BCG growth – share matrix displays the various busi-ness units on a graph of the market rate vs. market share rel-ative to competitors:

Market Share
HIGH   LOW

HIGH	Stars	Question Marks
LOW	Cash Cow	Dogs

Market Growth

Fig 10.2: BCG Growth - Share Matrix

Resources are allocated to business units according to where they are situated as follows:

A question mark (or problem child) is in a growing market but does not have a high market share. Its parent company may be spending heavily to increase the market share

A star is a product (or business) which has a high market share in a growing mar-ket. The business is able to break even and make profits though it spends heavily to increase the mar-ket share

A cash cow is a product (or business) with high market share in a mature market. Because growth is low and market condi-tions are more stable the need for heavy marketing investment is less. The cash cow is thus a cash provider

Dogs have a low market share and low market growth. They are cash drain

To portray alternative corporate growth strategies, Igor Ansoff presented a matrix that focused on the firm's present and potential product and markets (customers). By considering ways to grow via existing products and new products, and in existing markets and new markets, there are four possible prod-uctmarket combinations.

	EXISTING PRODUCTS	NEW PRODUCTS
EXISTING MARKETS	Market Penetration	Product Development
NEW MARKETS	Market Development	Diversification

Fig. 10.3: Ansoff Matrix

Ansoff's matrix provides four different growth strategies:

Market Penetration

The firm seeks to achieve growth with existing products in their current mar-ket segments, aiming to increase its market share. The market penetration strategy is the least risky since it leverages many of the firm's existing re-sources and capabilities. In a growing market, simply maintaining market share will result in growth and there may exist opportunities to increase market share if competitors reach capacity limits. However, market penetra-tion has limits, and once the market approaches saturation another strategy must be pursued if the firm is to continue to grow.

Market Development

The firm seeks growth by targeting its existing products to new market segments. Market development options include: the pursuit of additional market segments. The development of new market for the product may be a good strategy if the firm's core competencies are related more to the specific market segment. Because the firm is expanding into a new market the market development strategy typically has more risk than a market penetration strategy.

Product Development

The firm develops new products targeted to its existing market segments. A product development strategy may be appropriate if the firm's strengths are related to its specific customers rather than to the specific product itself. In this situation it can leverage the strengths by developing a new product targeted to its existing customers. Similar to the case of knew market development, new product development carries more risk than simply attempting to increase market share.

Diversification

The firm seeks to grow by diversifying into new businesses by developing new products for new markets. Diversification is the most risky of the four growth strategies since it requires both products and marketing development and may be out of the core competencies of the firm. In fact this quadrant of the matrix has been referred to by some as the "suicide cell". However, di-versification may be a reasonable choice if the high risk is compensated by the chance of high rate of return. Other advantages of diversification includethe potential to gain a foothold in an attractive industry and the reduction of overall business.

CHAPTER 9

The transition from an entrepreneurial style to a managerial approach

THE STRATEGY OF MOVING FROM SINGLE APPROACH TO A LEVEL OF EMPLOYING MANAGERS IS KEY TO BUSINESS GROWTH for example the transaction between stages of a venture are complemented (or in some cases retarded) by the entrepreneur's ability to make a transition in style. In many cases a key transition occurs during the growth stage of a venture when the entrepreneur shifts into a managerial style. In real sense this is not easy to do. One business guru says "among the different transitions that are possible, probably the most difficult to achieve and also perhaps the most important for organizational development is that of moving from one – person, entrepreneurially managed firm to one run by a functionally organized professional management team.

A number of problems can occur during this transition, especially if the enterprise is characterized by factors such as a highly centralized decision – making system, an overdependence on one or two key individuals, an inadequate repertoire of managerial skills and training, and a paternalistic atmosphere. These characteristics although often effective in the new venture's start – up and initial survival, pose a threat to the firm's development during the growth stage. Quite often these characteristics inhibit development by detracting from the entrepreneur's ability to manage the growth stage successfully.

In order to bring about the necessary transition, the entrepreneur must carefully plan and then gradually implement the process. The following seven steps are suggested:

1. The entrepreneur must want to make the change and must want it strongly enough to undertake major modifications in his or her own task behaviour.
2. The day to day decision – making procedures of the organization must be changed specifically and participation in the process must be expanded.
3. The two or three key operating tasks that are primarily responsible for the organization's success must be institutionalized. This may involve the selection of the new people to supplement or replace "indispensable" individuals who have performed these tasks in the past.
4. Middle level management must be developed. Specialists must learn to become functional managers, while functional managers must learn to become General Managers.
5. The firm's strategy should be evaluated and modified, if necessary to achieve growth.
6. The organizational structure and its management and procedures must be slowly modified to fit the company's new strategy and senior managers.
7. The firm must develop a professional board of directors.

HOW TO CHANGE YOUR MANAGEMENT STYLE

What Type of Manager Are You?

The first step to changing your management style is identifying what type of manager you are. Many management writers say that traditionally, there are four management styles, but a fifth is also worth noting.

Balancing the Focus (Entrepreneur and manager)

In managing the growth stage entrepreneurs must remember two important points: First, an adaptive firm needs to retain certain entrepreneurial characteris-tics in order to encourage innovation and creativity. Second, the entrepreneur needs to translate this spirit of innovation and creativity to his or her personnel while personally making a transition toward a more management style.

Despite many favourable attributes, the average small enterprise is often strug-gling for survival in a hostile environment. Lessons learnt in Africa show that the policy framework many times is to the disadvantage of the small entrepreneur. For example, in the case of Nigeria, recent studies disclose that import tariffs applied favour larger companies and the use of advanced technologies. In one case, large companies paid duties of between 0-10 per cent on the import value while small-scale competitors had to pay 30-65 per cent although they were pro-ducing identical or similar goods.

A result of the policy framework is that many entrepreneurs are tempted to use an inappropriate technology. They soon find themselves trapped in a situation they cannot manage. Limited technical skills means that maintenance will be poorly done and the machinery will deteriorate. Lack of spareparts and in some cases raw material for the production process due to foreign currency restrictions might halt the operation altogether.

Many businessmen running a small venture are also facing capital restrictions although not for investments in machinery and equipment. On the contrary, funds for investment in fixed assets are often easily accessible and in fact many small enterprises have a large unused capacity. The commonly encountered capital constraint is instead to get working capital. Indeed, very few sources are available to supply the small entrepreneur with money to buy raw material and intermediates, andto pay workers wages,.

Small-scale enterprises in the forest sector rarely exist with business as the single dominating activity of the owner/manager: the small business operation is carried out on part-time basis, often as a complement to agricultural activities. In many cases, assets are also used for several ventures. It is therefore very difficult to measure the real importance and productivity of the sector or to assist the forest-based activity in isolation. It is also noted that forest-based small enterprises of-ten are located where raw materials are available. Compared with other lines of business they tend to be more spread out and consequently more difficult to reach with traditional approaches and assistance such as management training and extension service.

Most forest-based small scale enterprises apply unsophisticated production methods and equipment. It seems that most work on an order basis rather than pro-ducing for stock to supply a distant market.

Although such a system reduces the working capital tied up in production or stock, it also limits the scope for pro-ductivity improvements.

It is of interest to note that early findings from an ILO-study presently being executed shows that the above-mentioned characteristics apply not only to the formal sector but also to forest-based businesses of the informal sector. A con-clusion that might be drawn from this is that when discussing needs for manage-ment improvements and assistance, there are few reasons for separating the analysis of small enterprises in the formal sector from that of the informal sector.

Management of small-scale enterprises

To avoid academic discussion, management is here simply defined as the way a commercial/business activity is organized. Before looking at the forest-based sector, discussed below are some general issues relating to small enterprise man-agement. While it is realised that management in small enterprises normally is personalised rather than being institutionalised, still the management of small enterprises can improve their position vis-a-vis competitors by introducing man-agement practices that give consistency and viability to the administration of the entire business.

The very ownership of a business tends to create elitist attitudes and self-orientation. It imposes a monocular vision which limits the company's capacity to respond positively and aggressively to business opportunities and changing business conditions. A person who stands head and shoulders over his colleagues in perceived authority can create benefits as well as disadvantages for the business. In cases where he is a poor manager even though a good entrepreneur, his domination might prevent the enterprise from obtaining the skills and methods which are needed for further growth. A gap is thus created between the manager/owner's perception of the situation and his own abilities on the one hand and of the actual needs of the business on the other.

Small enterprises often apply a minimum of formalisation. They achieve the output without much of differentiation in job content. The built-in informality facilitates a smooth response to minor disruptions but it renders at the same time excuses for not establishing and enforcing proper performance standards. Due to the informality of the business and to the fact that most small enterprises are op-erating with short product cycles, the managers/entrepreneurs do not conceptual-ise their situation in terms of opportunities, expertise or strength. The enterprise might as a consequence implement decisions on the basis of invalid assumptions or a misperception of the situation.

Discipline at workplace is affected in cases where a small enterprise is filled with relatives of the owner or manager, especially if there are elderly relatives since in many cultures it is difficult or even impossible to govern or reprimand such an older relative/employee. The extended family system, where it operates, requires that in the recruitment of employees for such a family business, relations of the owner/manager have to be considered irrespective of other employment criteria.

Since many entrepreneurs of small enterprises lack managerial experience when they start their business career, there is often a tendency of basing decisions and actions on hope and dreams rather than solid data. There are for example numer-ous cases of small enterprises going into bankruptcy because of the simple fact that they did not know how to price their goods or services. In such cases, even the introduction of the most basic management principles could improve the per-formance of the enterprises.

Many business commentators advocate the following characterises organisation and management of small enterprises:

- The entrepreneur succeeds in business due to his technical skills, not because of his ability to conceptualise market opportunities or plan ahead in strategic terms;
- In contrast to large companies, which can usually afford specialist staff, the small enterprise manager is a relatively isolated individual trying to deal with long-term policy issues and day-to-day operational problems simultaneously;
- Small enterprise managers often operate without adequate quantitative data or other information, rather following the strategy of other successful entrepreneurs;
- Due to low wages, limited job security and a low status from working in a small-scale enterprise, the manager cannot easily recruit and keep qualified employees.
- Due to these shortcomings, many small enterprises fail to adjust in response to environmental changes, introduction of new technology or similar developments. When the skills and experience of the owner/manager become outdated, the enterprise slips into stagnation.

Given the characteristics of small enterprises in the forest-sector, with many tiny units on the border between formal and informal sector supplementing the in-come of the entrepreneur's family, the need for management improvement are more basic or different from those of many other lines of business. Due to the informal and irregular manner in which operations are carried out, often as a complement to agricultural work, the financial flows of the enterprise are not separated from the economy of the family. Proper books and records are rarely maintained and the assets of the enterprise are not insured.

Making baskets - a family business

Many entrepreneurs in the forest sector also depend on limited market opportu-nities and produce few or a single product of a relatively low quality which ex-cludes them from operating on export markets. The often poor quality of prod-ucts is basically an effect of rudimentary tools and equipment being utilized. The use of relatives or poorly trained employees with low payment reinforces the quality problem. Especially in rural areas, qualified workers are not easily found.

Finally, in addition to low salaries, many small enterprises such as those in the forest sector offer poor working conditions and lack even the most basic safety-measures. This tends to increase the problem of experienced workers moving to larger enterprises in urban areas.

Entrepreneurship and management development issues related to the small en-terprise sector

Management support to the small enterprise sector covers the whole range of issues from identification/selection of entrepreneurs, initial management training, support through extension services and functional support to strengthening of small enterprise development agencies and development of national policies on promotion of small enterprises.

Many countries have training programmes for the small enterprise sector but lack a specific education and training policy for small enterprises development. A number of issues need to be resolved before policies can be implemented at the national level. In the first place, potential entrepreneurs have to be identified. Even when selection procedures are used, only a relatively small percentage of graduates actually start and succeed in business. Some experts believe that wasted effort and financial loss can best be avoided by a self-selection process whereby rigorous exercises completed before attending a formal training pro-gramme allow participants to judge their own entrepreneurial potential.

Another issue is to determine the appropriate level of training. Assuming that entrepreneurship can be induced, should the starting point for entrepreneurship development be the primary, secondary, post-secondary or post-tertiary education level? The answer to this question will depend to a certain extent on the type and level of training of the personnel involved in small enterprises development assistance. It is sometimes argued that including entrepreneurship training in the primary or secondary curriculum would mean devoting less attention to basic skills such as languages, mathematics and science. This is countered by those who maintain that entrepreneurial attitudes take a long time to develop and should therefore be taught as early as possible. One reason for introducing self-employment concepts to children at the primary level in developing countries is that many of them do not pursue their formal education at the secondary level. The cost of doing so would be minimal yet it would enable young people to be informed of the possibilities of self-employment as a career. An issue of interest is also whether early entrepreneurship training should be sector oriented in order to gear potential entrepreneurs towards expanding lines of business or if the training should be kept general.

In some industrialised countries, post-secondary educational institutions provide special training programmes for potential entrepreneurs. In the developing coun-tries, too, university-level business programmes sometimes cater to the specific needs of small enterprises. Governments are now having to decide whether to introduce basic changes in the educational system so as to offer business educa-tion and training for various age-groups.

Financing entrepreneurship development programmes is also an important issue.

In some countries, the entire cost is borne by the government, in others by the participants. The decision in this matter will depend to a large extent on the type of small enterprises being aimed at (modern small enterprises, craftworkers, informal sector entrepreneurs, self-employed women, etc.). As to whether the government or the private sector should be responsible for such programmes, opinions differ, some arguing that overall government control is essential to co-ordinate the programme and others that the government should not be involved in any part of the programme that can he carried out by the private sector. In some instances entrepreneurship development programmes are offered jointly by government and private sector organisations. There is considerable controversy, too, over whether the programme should stop at business creation and the par-ticipants be left entirely to their own ventures once they have received their initial training or whether, on the contrary, follow-up counselling and even other types of assistance such as credit should be available for the first year or two of operation of a new small enterprise as part of the programme.

Given the particular characteristics of the forest-based small enterprise sector with small, family based units distributed in rural areas, successful assistance programmes will probably differ considerably from most existing approaches. One key issue is whether to concentrate on those with the largest potential for entrepreneurship and assume that the local community will benefit eventually rather than using scarce resources to support income supplementing activities with little scope for improvement. Although very small income generating busi-ness ventures are important from the individual's point of view and contribute to employment and national production output, it can still be argued that due to the irregular nature of activities the productivity of assistance to such tiny units is less than that of support to somewhat larger and more permanent enterprises.

In the field of social science, during the past 50 years, extensive research has been carried out regarding the issue how human beings learn and acquire skills. Although much is known today about the learning process, relatively few research projects have focused on how successful businessmen obtained their en-trepreneurial and managerial skills. Available evidence indicates that the devel-opment of entrepreneurial and managerial skills is a process different from most other learning. The importance of the childhood, early experience from working life as well as an environment favourable to business ventures are all ingredients necessary for the development of entrepreneurial attitudes and talents. Although the issue whether entrepreneurship can be taught or is inherited is still debated, there is today fairly strong support for the assumption that such traits can be de-veloped through well designed training programmes as will be further discussed below.

When it comes to development of managerial skills, the issue is not whether they can be transferred by training but rather to what extent the quality of training programmes can be improved to the level where they attract the attention of hard-working entrepreneurs. A vast number of small business training institutions throughout the world are offering more or less comprehensive training pro-grammes geared towards the local business community. Many of these efforts fail, often because the programme design is poor. Too many programmes are containing over-sophisticated components and abstract training materials far from the reality of the entrepreneur. In many cases, the programmes are also over -ambitious in terms of the commitment expected from the entrepreneurs. Few successful, or moderately successful entrepreneurs can manage to stay away from their businesses for long periods, something which is unfortunately often not taken into account among training officers designing the programmes.

PART III

Corporate Entrepreneurship

CHAPTER 10

Money Management

MONEY MANAGEMENT OR FINANCIAL MANAGEMENT is one of the important disciplines among others such as marketing management, operations management, human resource management and procurement. Money management or financial management as it is commonly called is that branch of management accounting which deals with the management of finances in order to achieve the financial objectives of an organization. It deals with the acquisition and allocation of resources among firms, the firm's present and po-tential activi-ties and projects" Acquisition is concerned with the "financial decision", the gen-eration of funds internally or exter-nally at lowest possible cost. Allocation is concerned with the "investment decision", the use of these funds to achieve cor-po-rate financial objectives.

Financial Objectives

The conventional assumption is that most trading organiza-ions' objective is the maximization of the value of the company or business for its owners. Since the owners of a company are its shareholders, the primary objective of a trading company is said to be "the maximization of shareholders' wealth. The wealth comes from dividends received by the shareholders and the market value of the business, that is, capital gains from increases in market value. In achieving this objective, other objectives are suggested due to the existence of other interest groups with stakes in the company including, leaders, employees, the community at large, government etc. It must be emphasized though that while companies do have to consider other stakeholders, from a corporate finance perspective, such objectives should only consider other stakeholders, from a corporate finance perspective, such objectives should only be pursued in support of the overriding long-term objective of maximizing shareholders' wealth. Modern finance theory usually assumes that the objective of the firm is to maximize the wealth of share-holders.

Other possible objectives of the business include: Maximizing Profits Market Share, Obtaining Greater "Managerial Power", Increasing Employee Welfare, Increasing Social Responsibility, and Corporate Growth. These objectives are operative but tend to be less important than maximizing shareholders' wealth.

Agency Theory

Large corporations characterized by separation of ownership and control. This may lead to conflicts between management and shareholders. Conflicts may also arise between: Group of bondholders for example subordinated versus unsubordinated + debt) Groups of shareholders, Bond holders and shareholders, Management Personnel (scarce corporate resources).

Management Vs Shareholders

It should be clear that the corporation can be viewed as a complicated set of contractual relationships among individuals. It should be noted that, equity is a Residential Claim. As owners of the corporation the relationship with management is one of PRINCIPAL – AGENT. It is assumed that, left alone man-agers and shareholders will each attempt to act in their own interest. Thus managers have day-to-day operational control of the firm. Manager's goal is the maximization of a "Corporate Wealth", in other words the wealth over which management has control. Corporate Wealth is not equal to shareholder wealth.

Agency Costs

These are costs associated with resolving the conflicts of interest between man-agers and shareholders for example audit costs. There is however a trade – off between the costs and benefits of controlling management. Agency costs also incur when managers do not attempt to maximize firm value and shareholders in -cur costs to monitor the managers and influence their actions. There are no costs when the shareholders are also managers. Owner manager has no conflict of interest. This is one of the advantages of sole proprietorship.

Financial Institutions and Financial Markets

Financial Institutions are financial intermediaries that accept deposits from savers and invest in capital markets. Their functions range from accepting deposits, pay-ment mechanism, borrowing and lending and pooling risks. Classes of these inter -mediaries include: deposit institutions. such as banks, insurance companies, trust companies. and money managers, credit union and Mutual Funds. The financial systems within the financial institutions include: People (Investors and Borrow-ers), Place (Markets), Product (Securities and Treasury Bills), Price (Cost of Capital and Cost of Borrowing or simply interest

Capital Markets

Capital Markets or Financial Markets as they are commonly called are markets that manage the surplus units and deficit units. e.g. Those that have money will invest in the capital/financial market. Similarly those that do not have will go and borrow from these markets.

Objectives of the capital markets include: providing link between companies raising funds for their expansion and people with funds to invest. Providing a market place for buying and selling of shares at market determined price.

Supervising trad-ing activities so as to ensure that the interests of customers are looked after and are carried out fairly properly according to the governing rules of exchange.

Treasury Functions

Treasury Management is the corporate handling of all financial matters, the gen-eration of internal and external funds of the business, the management of curren-cies and cash flows and complex strategies, policies and procedures of corporate fi-nance. Liquid management making sure that the firm has liquid funds it needs. Funding management concerned with all forms of borrowing and alternative sources of funds such as leasing and factoring, bank loans and debentures,.

Currency management exposure policies and procedures for example Interna-tional monetary economics. Corporate finance, equity, capital management, business acquisitions and sales and project finance. Maintaining relationship with banks, stock-holders and other investors who hold the firms securities.

Centralised cash management has some advantages. For example it avoids hav-ing a mix of cash surpluses and overdrafts in different localized bank accounts. Larger volumes of cash are available to invest giving better short term opportu-nities such as treasury bills. Any borrowing can be arranged in bulk at lower interest rates than for smaller borrowings. So too the decentralized cash manage-ment has advantages: sources of finance can be diversified and can match local assets. Greater autonomy can be given to subsidiaries and is more responsive to the needs of individuals operating units.

Cost of Funds

When you get a loan from a bank, the bank charges interest on the loan. The interest that you get is the cost of lending the money. In other words, the bank could put the money to other use and earn a profit equivalent to or more than the interest that you pay on the loan. Cost of funds or the minimum re-quired return a company should make on its own investments, to earn the cash flows out of which investors can be paid their return. Therefore cost of capital is the minimum acceptable return on an investment.

Cost of funds has three elements. First, the risk free-rate – this is the return one would get if a security was completely free of any risk. Second, risk free yields are typically on government securities, for example yields on Treasury Bills and third, the premium for business risk – this is an increase in the required rate of return due to compensate for existence of uncertainty about the future of a busi-ness.

Cost of funds can be cost of equity or cost of debt. Cost of equity could be esti-mated by dividend valuation model, which is based on the fundamental analysis theory. This theory states that the market value of shares is directly related to expected future dividends on the shares. The cost of debt capital already issued is the rate of interest (the internal rate of return), which equates the current mar-ket price with the discounted future cash receipts from the security.

Weighted Average Cost of Capital

In most cases, a company's funds may be viewed as a pool of resources that is, a combination of different funds with differ-ent costs. Under such circumstances it might seem appropriate to use an average cost of capital for investment approval. High level of debt creates financial risk. Financial risk is measured by gearing ratio.

$$\frac{D}{E + D}$$

Higher gearing will increase KE (cost of equity) Where D stands for Debt and E stands for equity. As the level of gearing increase the cost of debt remain un-changed up to the certain level of gearing. The Ke (cost of equity) rises as the level of gear-ing increases (need for higher returns). The WACC does not remain constant but rather falls initially as the proportion of debt increases and then begins to increase as the rising cost of equity/debt becomes more significant. The optimum level of gearing is where the company's weighted cost of capital is minimized. This assumes that WACC is unchanged because of the following two factors: Cost of debt remains unchanged on the level of gear-ing increases. Cost of equity rises in such a way as to keep the WACC constant.

Cash Flow Forecasting

A business has a responsibility to make payments when they are due regardless of whether sufficient cash has been collect-ed from customers to provide the means of payment. Unpaid suppliers may be begrudgingly tolerant and wait a little longer for their cash, but they may refuse to fulfil further orders until payment is made and they may even take legal action to recover to debt. This requires the corporation to prepare cash flow statements.

Cash Flow Statement presents financial adaptability. It is a statement of cash inflows and cash out flows. On one hand key cash inflows include: Cash Sales, Receipts from debtors coming as a function of credit sales: This means the Fi-nance Department must have a strong credit control section which should intensify on debt collection; Sell of Fixed Assets such as Vehicles, Furniture, com-puters and Equipment among others and other such as donations or grants.

On the other hand cash out flows include: Payment of Cred-itors, Payments to Lenders of Finance, Administrative Expenses such as salaries, rentals, insurance among others, Dividend Pay Out, Taxation such as corporate tax, Purchase of Fixed As-sets such as Vehicles, Furniture, computers and Equipment, Invest-ments into projects and other business portfolios. To enable management to plan appropriately and feel confident that payments can be made as they fall due, a detailed cash flow forecast is required that predicts timing and amounts of re-ceipts and payments. The advance warning of any potential cash shortages that are revealed allows management the time. to put together a considered rather than active, plan for bridg-ing any gaps in cash flow. It can take time to negoti-ate with the banks and raise additional finance and with a well-structured and realistic cash flow forecast this can be done well in advance of any potential need.

Furthermore, a well – constructed cash flow forecast helps banks and other providers of finance confidence in management realism and competence.

Table 12:1 A cash flow forecast

	Month 1	Month 2	Month 3	Month 4	Month 5
Opening Balance	6,000	5,200	6,400	(1,500)	(2,000)
Receipts	8,300	(12,600)	4,900	8,800	11,600
Payments	(9,100)	(11,400	(12,800)	(9,300)	(9,200)
Closing Balance	5,200	6,400	1,500)	(2,000)	400

Source: Ngwira(2015)

Table 12:1 above shows that there is a mismatch in receipts and payments that creates a deficit in months 3 and 4. These need to be recovered by one or more of the following: cash invest-ment; the use of overdraft facility (a temporary loan). The defer-ral of purchases or payments that falls due in 3 and 4 such as acquisition of assets and the acceleration of receipts that arrive in month 5 (perhaps by offering discounts for early settlement.

Investment Opportunities

Investment of cash involves selecting the right assets at the right time at right price. Most Capital Investment Decisions will have a direct effect on future prof-itability either because they will result in an increase in revenue or because they will bring about an increase in efficiency and a reduction in costs. What-ever level of management authorizes a capital expenditure the proposed investment should be properly evaluated and found to be worthwhile, before the decision is taken to go ahead with the expenditure.

Capital expenditure differ from day to day revenue expenditure for the following reasons: They often involve a bigger outlay of money; the benefits will accrue over a long period of time, usually over a period over one year and often much longer This means that the benefits can not be set against costs in the current year's profit and loss account.

The Accounting Rate of Return (ARR)

The Accounting Rate of Return method of appraising a capi-tal project is to estimate the ARR or Return on Investment (ROI) that the project should yield a return that exceeds a target rate of return then that project can be undertaken

ARR = Estimated Average Profits X 100
Estimated Average Investments

Payback Period

When deciding between two or more competing projects the usual decision is to accept the one with shortest payback period. Pay back is commonly used as the first screening method to ascertain how long will it take to pay back its cost? The organization might have a target pay back and so it would reject a capital project unless its payback period is less than a certain number of years depending on the company policy.

However, a project should not be evaluated on the basis of payback alone. The pay back method should be a first screening process and if a project passes the pay back test it aught then to be evaluated using another investment appraisal technique. The reason why pay back should not be used on its own to evaluate capital investments should be always be clear.

Discounted Cash Flow

As noted above the ARR method of project evaluation ignores the timing of cash flows and the opportunity cost of capital tied up. Payback considers the time it takes to recover the original investment cost, but ignores total profits over a project's life. The DCF is an investment appraisal technique which takes into account both the timing value of money and also total profit-ability over a project-life. So DCF is superior to both ARR and Payback as the timing of cash flows is taken into account by discounting them

Internal Rate of Return

The IRR is to calculate the exact rate of return which the project is expected to achieve that is the discount rate at which the NPV is 0. If the expected rate of return exceeds the target rate of return the project should be undertaken.

$$\frac{a + x \times (b\text{-}a)}{x - y}$$

- a is a lower rate of return and b is the higher rate of re-turn
- X is the + NPV
- Y is the - NPV The following cash flows have been estimated for a project: Year Cash Flow (MK'000)
  0   (MK2000)

  1   400

  2   600

3   700

4   600

5   500

It is required to calculate the project NPIWe need to state whether the project is acceptable assuming that the cost of capital is either: 10% or 20 %.

(a) NPV when the cost of capital is 10%

2000 + (400x0.909) + (600x0.826) + (700x0.751) + (600x.683) + (500x.621) = + MK105

(b) NPV when cost of capital is 20%

2000 + (400x0.833) + (600x0.694) + (700x0.579) + (600x.482) + (500x.402) = - MK355 a + x x (b-a)
x − y = 10% + 105 x (20-10) 105 - - 355 = 12.3%

CHAPTER 11

Operations Management

Stevenson in his book "Operations Management" he points out that opera-tions management involves planning, coordinating, and executing of all activities that create goods or provide services. The subject matter is fascinating and timely; productivity, quality, foreign competition, and customer service are very much in the news. All are part of production and operations management. Production is the process of converting, or transforming resources into goods or services.

Resources include materials, machines, employees, time, methods, management, information and money. The output of the production process may be manufactured goods and other services. Therefore Production & Operations Management may be defined in the areas of design, operation and improvement of the production systems that create the firm's primary product of rservices.

Like Marketing and finance, Operations Management. is functional field of busi-ness with clear line management responsibilities. The term operations describe the set of all activities associated with the production of goods and services. Op-erations may involve manufacturing, in which goods are physically created from material inputs, transportation, in which the location of something or someone is changed; supply, in which the ownership or possession of goods is changed; or service, in which the principal characteristic is the treatment or accommodation to something or someone.

The management of operations – that is, the planning, organizing, and control-ling of the production process and the management of the interface with supporting functions in the organization is called

Production and Operations Management (P/OM) or simply Operations Management.

Operations Management

You may be wondering why you need to know the importance of Operations Management. Actually, there are these very good reasons: one is that Operations Management activities are at the core of all business organizations regardless of what business they are in. It is therefore one of the major functions of any organization and is essential to understand what organizations do.

We understand how people organize themselves for productive enterprise. Be-cause we want to know how goods and services are produced. The production function is the segment of our society that creates products we use. Because pro-duction operations management is on the mostly costly parts of any organization. Production and Operations Management help us understand what production and operations managers do.

By understanding what these managers do can build the decision-making skills necessary to be such a manager. For example 35 percent or more of all jobs are in operations management related areas such areas as customer service, quality as-sur-ance, production planning and control, scheduling job design, inventory man-agement and many more.

Activities in all of the other areas of business organizations, such as finance, ac-counting, human resources, logistics marketing, purchasing as well as others are all interrelated with operations management activities, so it is essential for these people to have a basic understanding of operations management. But beyond all of this is the reality that production/operations management is about manage-ment, and all managers need to possess the knowledge and skills in the content areas you will learn about here. Among them are productivity, strategy, fore-casting, quality, inventory control, and scheduling,. Also you will learn how to use a range of quantitative tools to enhance man-agerial decision making. Many believe that reversing the trend in manufacturing competitiveness requires more effective management of operations.

Operations management is now "where the action is". Only a few people have chosen careers in that area. There is now a shortage of skilled managers who un-derstand the critical issues in P/OM. The service sector represents the most rapidly grow-ing segment of the workforce. Issues of productivity and quality in providing services have become increasingly important. Fig. 13.1: Input Transformation Output Model 1

THE INPUT TRANSFORMATION OUT PUT MODEL

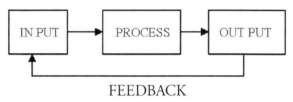

FEEDBACK
Source: Ngwira (2015)
Fig. 13.2: Input Transformation Output Model 2
Input—Transformation—Output Processes

INPUT
- Transforming Resources
- The resources that are treated, transformed or converted in some way
- These include information and customers
- Transforming Resources
- The resources that act upon the transformed resources

COMPETITIVE PRIORITIES

Entrepreneurs require to have a thorough understanding of competitive priorities which should make their ventures competitive than their rivals. The following are the performance objectives or competitive priorities which if put into action will put your business a head of competition and you will be able to stay in the busi-ness game longer:
- Quality
- Time (Speed Advantage) – Faster Customer Response

Facilities and staff: Facilities include buildings, equipment and technology while staff include those who operate, maintain, plan and manage the operations.

TRANSFORMATION PROCESS

Operations Strategy – the total patterns of decisions and actions which set the role, objectives and activities of the operations so that they contribute to and sup-port the organization's business strategy.
- Improvement
- Design
- Planning and Control OM is therefore a function that manages the resources that add value.
- Flexibility (Variety and More Innovation)
- Dependability (On Time Deliveries)
- Cost (Doing Business Cheaply)

Operations Strategy

Many companies neglected to include operations strategy in their corporate strat-egy. Some of them paid dearly for that neglect. Now more and more companies are recognizing the im-portance of operations strategy on the overall success of their business, and the necessity for relating it to their overall business strategy. Total Quality Management (TQM) – Many firms are now adopting a total qual-ity management approach to their business. Under this approach, the entire or-ganization from the chief executive down becomes committed to, and involved in, a never-ending quest to improve the quality of goods and services. Key fea-tures often include a team approach, finding and eliminating problems, emphasis on serving the customer, and continuously working to improve the system.

Flexibility – The ability to adapt quickly to changes in volume of demand, in the mix of products demanded, and in product design, has become a major competi-tive strategy in manufac-turing, the term agile manufacturing is sometimes used to connote flexibility.

Time reduction – Many companies are focusing efforts on reducing the time needed to accomplish various tasks in order to gain a competitive edge. If two companies can provide the same product at the same price and quality, but one can deliver it four weeks earlier than the other, the quicker company will in-variably get the sale.

Time reductions - are being achieved in processing, informaation retrieval, product design, and the response to customer complaints.

Technology – Technological advances have led to a vast array of new products and processes. The computer has had, and will continue to have the greatest im-pact on business organizations. It has truly revolutionized the way companies operate. Applications include product design, product features, processing tech-nology, information processing and communication. Technological advances in new materials, new methods, and new equipment have also made their mark on operations.

Technological changes in products and processes can have major implications for production systems, affecting competitiveness and quality, but unless technology is carefully inte-grated into an existing system, it can do more harm than good by raising costs, reducing flexibility, and even reducing productivity.

Worker involvement – More and more companies are pushing the responsibility for decision making and problem solving to lower levels in the organization. The reasons for this trend include recognition of the knowledge workers possess about the production process and the contributions they can make to improve the production system. A key to worker involvement is the use of teams of workers who solve problems and make decisions on a consensus basis.

Reengineering – Some companies are taking drastic measures to improve their performance. They are conceptually starting from scratch in redesigning their processes. Business reengi-neering means starting over, asking why a company does things the way it does, and questioning basic rules and assumptions. Engi-neering focuses on significantly improving business pro-cesses, such as the steps required to fill

Corporate downsizing – Squeezed by competition, lagging productivity and stockholders calling for improved profits and share prices, many corporations have responded by reducing their labour forces. This has meant that operations managers often have to find ways to produce more with fewer workers. Supply chain management – Organizations are increasing their attention to managing the supply chain, from suppliers and buyers of raw materials all the way to final cus-tomers. Lean Production – Incorporates a number of the recent trends listed here, with an emphasis on quality, flexibility, time reduction, and teamwork. This has led to a flattering of the organizational structure with fewer levels of management.

The activities of operations managers in business include: Planning and Control; Capacity ; Design; Improvement; Location; producing products (goods and ser-vices); Make or buy decisions; deciding on facilities layout; managing projects and scheduling among others.

CHAPTER 12

Marketing Management

MARKETING IS IMPORTANT FUNCTION in the operation of a com-pany. Marketing is concerned with making profits by providing customer satisfac-tion. Thus when people buy products or services they do not want the products or service per se, they want the benefits from using the products or services. Products and services help to solve customers' problems. It is the solu-tions to these problems that customers are really buying.

What is marketing?

Marketing is defined as the process of planning and executing conception, pric-ing, promotion and distribution of ideas, goods and services to create exchanges that satisfy individual and organizational goals. Marketing is the performance of ac-ivities that seek to accomplish an organization's objectives by anticipating customer or client needs and directing a flow of need satisfying goods and ser-vices from producer to custom-er or client. Marketing is the management process responsible for identifying, anticipating and satisfying consumers' requirements profitably. Therefore marketing is more than selling and advertising.

Once you have basics right, one can now embark on sales and marketing. No business can succeed without making sales. Generate new clients while keeping retaining and grow existing ones. Remember the bird in your hand is better than the ones flying in the air. Business is about repeat business. Treat your custom-ers/clients with respect as if your business cannot do without them. While you chase the new customers do not forget the existing ones. There must be people that go out to sell. This is a call to create a brand, business name, identity, logo, fliers, brochures that have information about your product. Design letter heads, business cards.

Do Market research on product, market, customers and net-working/ socialize as an excellent way of getting customers. Come up with a name that separates you from the rests. Build business with long term relationships. Without relationships there is no business especially repeat business. Remember that customer service is what keeps the client in your books. A cus-tomer is the reason for our existence. Without that customer you will be out of business.

Development of Present Day Marketing

In early industrial and commercial developments the em-phasis was placed on production. Demand was high and all that was manufactured could be sold with-out difficulty. Later the emphasis switched to sales. With reduction in consumer demand, effort had to be made to sell factory output. Roughly the period from the 1920s to the 1950s, was characterized by this sales orientation. Thus sales and advertising were the ac-tivities receiving most emphasis. Later from the 1950s to the present day with ever increasing competitor activity and con-sumer needs and wants should initiate the production process.

Thus a marketing orientation developed and this is the current situation. How-ever, it is important to recognize that not all organizations adapted the marketing orientation and in most cases corporate failure can be directly attributed to com-panies having a production orientation approach. On one hand busi-nesses that have production orientation have the following characteristics: demand is a func-tion of supply: there is an emphasis on production, the firm has an inward looking approach, most things made can be sold, buyers are sensitive to price, market must have low cost, with sales orientation, selling the output of production be-came the most important activity. On the other hand businesses that follow mar-ket orientation have the following characteristics: they have scarcity of markets, have a focus on customers, have an outward looking approach, have high level of competitor activity and their supply exceeds demand.

Organizations adopting a marketing orientation or the mar-keting concept are therefore interested in the satisfaction of consumer needs and wants at a profit

Market Concept

Marketing concept is concerned with satisfying consumer needs and wants at a profit. Therefore business is about satisfying customers at a profit. So any com-pany implementing the marketing concept will achieve their corporate objectives by identifying and satisfying the needs and want of a target markets more effec-tively than competitors. Effective marketing starts with the recognition of cus-tomer needs and then works backwards to devise products or services to satisfy these needs.

In this way marketing managers can satisfy customers more efficiently in the present and anticipate changes in customer needs more accurately in the future. This means that organiza-tions should focus on building long term customer relations in which the initial sale is viewed as a beginning step in the process, not as an end goal.

Marketing Mix

Marketing involves making a number of interrelated decisions about various aspects of company activity, which have a major impact on success or failure of the company as a busi-ness enterprise. The term marketing mix is used to denote the range of activities within the framework of marketing decision making. The marketing mix is the set of controllable variables that must be managed to sat-isfy the target market and achieve organizational objectives.

For convenience, the market mix is divided into four major decision areas: Product, Price, promotion and Place decisions.

1. Product Decisions

These include the number, type, brand grouping and quality of company prod-ucts, their sizes, variety and form of packing. Decisions on whether to add new products, phase out products, restyle or rebrand fall into this category

2. Price Decisions

These include the discount structure, the relationship of price between product sizes, the general pricing policy and the pricing of new products.

3. Promotion Decisions

These include advertising strategy, media selection, copy writing, public relations, personal selling and special sales promotions, all involving the conveyance of information about the company.

4. Place Decisions

These include decisions relating to the distribution channels and the appointment of agents among other things. The effective use of the marketing tools within the marketing mix is an interrelated manner and is the key to successful marketing and profitable business. The aim of marketing management is to get the right product of the right quality to right place at the right price using the right promo-tional methods. Marketing management is therefore the process of putting into practice the marketing mixknown as the 4Ps.

To manage this process involves analysis, planning and control. As we have seen marketing orientation begins and ends with the customer. Thus analysis in mar-keting management involves finding the answers to the following questions: Who are our customers and potential customers? Who do they buy (or not buy). Do they buy our product or service? When do they buy it? Where do they buy it? How do they buy it? Having bought the product are they satisfied with it? How customers needs are changing? Which of the competitor's products do they con-sider buying? Marketing management also involves using the infor-mation gained from market analysis to plan the organization's marketing response/ activities. The third main component of marketing management is to control the operationalization of the marketing plan. Control involves setting measurable tar-gets for the plan and then checking performance against these targets. If neces-sary remedial action will need to be taken to ensure that planned and actual per-formances are brought into line.

Internal Marketing

As part of the overall marketing process of delivering customer satisfaction it is important that the whole corporate effort is coordinated and committed to achieving this objective. In practice this means that all employees at all levels should appreciate not only the reason for the firm's existence; but also that each and every employee has a responsibility to under-stand the concept of customer or marketing orientation and the importance of their individual contribution.

How Marketing Relates to Production

Although production is a necessary economic activity, some people overrate its importance in relation to marketing. Produc-tion and marketing are both impor-tant parts of a total busi-ness system aimed at providing consumers with need-satisfying 147 goods and services. Simply put take out marketing there will be no production. As stated in chapter 13 together, production and marketing supply five kinds of economic utility.

Form Utility: Form Utility is provided when someone produces something tangible (things you can touch or see)

Task Utility: Task Utility is provided when someone per-forms a task for some-one else. Thus marketing decisions focus on the customer and include decisions about what goods and services to produce. It does not make sense to provide goods and services consumers don't want when they are so many things they do want. Marketing is concerned with what customers want – and should guide what is produced and offered. Even when marketing and production combine to provide form or task utility, consumers will not be satisfied until possession, time and place utility are also provided.

Possession Utility: Possession utility means obtaining a product or service and having the right to use or consume it.

Time Utility: Time Utility means having the product avail-able when the cus-tomer wants.

Place Utility: Place utility means having the product available where the cus-tomer wants.

Market Strategy Planning

Market Strategy Planning means finding attractive opportu-nities and developing profitable marketing strategies. Marketing Strategy what is it? A market strategy specifies a target market and a related marketing mix. A target market is a fairly homoge-neous (similar) group of customers to whom a company wishes to ap-peal

Marketing Plan

The marketing plan is a guide to implementation and control. Marketing plan fills out marketing strategy. A market strategy sets a target market and a marketing mix. So a marketing plan is a written statement of a marketing strategy and the time related details for carrying out the strategy. Thus the marketing plan should spell out: what marketing mix will be offered; to whom (the target market) and for how long. What company resources will be needed at what rate and the plan should also include some control procedures.

After the marketing plan is developed, a marketing manag-er knows what needs to be done. The marketing manager is concerned with implementation – putting marketing plans into operation. Control is simply analysing and correcting what you have done. Therefore at the heart of the market plan we find situation analy-sis, marketing Objectives, target market selec-tion, market mix (The 4Ps of marketing) and implementation and control.

Marketing activities must be aligned with organizational ob-jectives and Market-ing opportunities are often found by sys-tematically analysing situation environ-ments. Once an oppor-tunity is recognized, the marketing manager must then plan an appropriate strategy for taking advantage of the opportunity. This process can be viewed in terms of: establishing marketing objectives, selecting the target market and developing the mar-keting mix.

What are the attractive opportunities?

There are breakthrough opportunities. These help innovators to develop hard to copy marketing strategies that will be very profitable for along time and enhance competitive advantage, marketing penetration, marketing development, product development, diversification strategies. International Opportunities should be considered (Getting an advantage of internationalization). For the market to be attractive should show competitiveness, effectiveness, should be robust and con-sistent.

Establishing the Market Objectives

Marketing objectives are usually derived from organizational objectives. Mar-keting objectives are stated as standards of performance.

A certain percentage of market share or sales volume). While such objectives are useful, the marketing concept emphasizes the profits rather than sales should be overriding objectives providing the framework for the marketing plan.

The Marketing Objectives

Market objectives include: increase the market share, continuity of profits, enlarging the market, harvesting and establishing market position.

Selecting Target Market

The success of any marketing plan hinges on how well it can identify customer needs and organize its resources to satisfy them profitably. Four important ques-tions must be answered: what do customers want and need? What must be done to sat-isfy these wants? What is the size of the market? What is the growth pro-file?

Getting Information for Marketing Decision

Marketing managers need information for implementation and control. Without good information managers will be forced to guess which is detrimental in to-day's fast changing markets. Information goes at a price and in some cases pro-viders of the information (customers and competitors) can be unpredictable. The manager should therefore decide what information is critical and how to get it. Marketing information systems (M.I.S) is an organized way of continually gath-ering and analysing data to provide marketing managers with the information they need to make decisions.

Relationship Marketing

A marketing orientation focuses on the needs of a customer first of all. Relation-ship marketing emphasizes the view that companies survive and prosper by sell-ing more goods to the same customer. Customers that purchase regularly develop expecations of the supplier. A customer must be turned from a one off purchaser to an advocate. The underlying principle of relationship marketing is that repeat business is more profitable. It costs less to sell to existing customers.

Market Research

The concept of marketing says that marketing managers should meet the needs of customers. Research provides a bridge to customers and this means marketing managers have to rely on help from marketing research. Marketing research in-volves procedures to develop and analyse new information which will help mar-keting managers to make decisions. Effective researches requires cooperation between marketing managers and researchers and of Ethical issues exist in mar-keting research and have to be considered by marketing managers in their deci-sions.

Market Research and the Scientific Method

Scientific method is a decision making approach that focuses on being objective and orderly in testing ideas before accepting them. Managers do not assume that their intuition is correct. They rather use their intuition and observations to de-velop a hypothesis. In simple terms a hypothesis is an educated guess about the relationships between things or about what will happen in the future. The hy-pothesis is then tested before making final decision. Scientific method helps mar-keting managers to make better decision. Marketing research includes the follow-ing five steps: defining the problem; analysing the situation; getting problem specif-ic data; interpreting the data and solving the problem.

CHAPTER 13

People Management

THE PRACTICE OF PEOPLE MANAGEMENT is concerned with all aspects of how people are employed and managed in organizations. It covers activities such as strategic Human Resource Management; human capital management; corporate social responsibility; knowledge management, organization management; resourcing (human resource planning, recruit-ment and selection and talent management); performance management; learning and development; reward management; Employee relations; Health and safety and Provision of employee services.

For the purposes of this chapter we will use the term Human Resource Manage-ment interchangeably with the term people management.

Human Resource Management Defined

A plethora of human resource management definitions has emerged: Stone in his book entitled Human Resource Management defines Human Resource Manage-ment as a productive use of people to achieve strategic business objectives and satisfy individual employee needs. According to Armstrong (2009) Human Re-source Management is a strategic, integrated and coherent approach to the em-ployment, development and well being of the people working in organizations.

However, other scholars say that human resource management involves all man-agement decisions and action that affect the nature of the relationship between the organization and its employees – its human resources. Boxall et al (2007) describe HRM as the management of work and people towards desired ends. Storey (1989) concurs with Boxall et al (2007) by believing that HRM can be regarded as a set of interrelated policies with an ideological and philosophical underpinning.

This means that HRM comprises a set of policies designed to maximise organizational integration, employee commitment, flexibility and quality of work. Therefore it can be concluded that HRM consists of the following propositions:

- That human resource policies should be integrated with strategic business planning.
- That human resource management is a distinct approach to employment man-agement which seeks to achieve competitive advantage through the strategic deployment of a highly committed and capable workforce.
- That HRM is concerned with how organizations manage their workforce.

Aims of HRM

The overall purpose of human resource management is to ensure that the organi-zation is able to achieve success through people. As Ulrich and Lake remark: 'HRM systems can be source of organizational capabilities that allow firms to learn and capitalize on new opportunities.

Personnel Vs. HRM

HRM is long term or proactive while Personnel Management is Short Term and Reactive. HRM is strategic while Personnel Management is Adhoc. HRM is Uni-tarist (focuses on an individual) while Personnel Management is pluralist and collective. HRM is Organic while Personnel Management is bureaucratic. HRM is largely integrated into line management while Personnel Management is specialist.

HR Strategies

The concept of strategy is based on a number of associated concepts: competitive advantage, resource – based strategy, distinctive capabilities, strategic intent, strategic capability, strategic management, strategic goals and strategic plans.

Competitive Advantage

The concept of competitive advantage was formulated by Michael Porter (1985). Competitive advantage, Porter asserts arises out of a firm creating value for its customers. To achieve it, firms select markets in which they can excel and present a moving target to their competitors by continually improving their position. Porter emphasized the importance of generic strategies (low cost leadership, differentiation and focus) the or-ganization can use to gain competitive advantage.

Distinctive Capabilities

As Kay comments, 'The opportunity for companies to sustain competitive ad-vantage is determined by their capabilities. A distinctive capability or compe-tence can be described as an important feature that confers superiority on the organization. Kay extends this definition by emphasizing that there is a dif-ference between distinctive capabilities and reproducible capabilities

On one hand distinctive capabilities are those characteristics that cannot be repli-cated by competitors or can only be imitated with great difficulty. On the other hand reproducible capabilities are those that can be bought or created by any com-pany with reasonable management skills, diligence and financial resources.

Prahaland and Hamel argue that competitive advantage stems in the long term when a firm builds core competences that are superior to those of its rivals and when it learns faster and applies its learning more effectively than its competi-tors. Distinctive capabilities or core competences describe what the organization is specially or uniquely capable of doing

Strategic Intent

In its simplest form, strategy could be described as an expression of the inten-tions of the organization – what it means to do and how. This means that busi-ness means to get from here to there. Strategic intent refers to the expression of the leadership position the organization wants to attain and establishes a clear criterion on how progress towards its achievement will be measured.

Strategic Capability

Strategic capability is a concept that refers to the ability of an organization to develop and implement strategies that will achieve sustained competitive advan-tage. It is therefore about the capacity to define realistic intentions, to match re-sources to opportunities and to prepare and implement strategic plans. People who display high levels of strategic capability know where they are going and know how they are going to get there.

Resource Based View

The resource – based view of strategy is that the strategic capability of a firm depends on its resource capability. It is important to know that competitive suc-cess does not come simply from making choices in the present. It stems from building up distinctive capabilities over significant periods of time.

What are HR Strategies

HR strategies set out what the organization intents to do about its human resource management policies and practices and how they should be integrated with the business strategy. They are defined by Dyer and Reeves as 'internally consistent bundles of human resource practices'. The purpose of HR strat-egies is to articu-late what an organization intends to do about its human resource management policies and practices now and in longer term. This means that business and man-agers should perform well in the present to succeed in the future. Thus, HR strategies aim to meet both business and human needs in the organization.

However, because all organizations are different, all HR strategies are different. There is no such a thing as a standard strategy and research into HR Strategy conducted by Armstrong and Long revealed many variations. Some strategies are simply very general declarations of intent.

Purpose of HR Strategy

To articulate what an organization intends to do about its human resource man-agement policies and practices now and in long term. General HR Strategy Areas include: High Performance Management; High Committed Management; High involvement of Management; Human Capital Management; Corporate Social Responsibility; Organization Development; Engagement; Knowledge Manage-ment; Employee Resourcing and Talent Management; Learning and Development; Reward; Employee Relations and Employee – Wellbeing.

How HR Strategies Can Be Implemented

To implement HR Strategies there is need to analyse business needs and how the HR Strategy will help to meet them. Then communicate full information on the strategy and what it is expected to achieve. You also need to involve those con-cerned in identifying implementation problems and how they should be dealt with in line with action plans. Finally, plan and execute a programme of project management that ensures that action plans are achieved.

Barriers to the Implementation of HR Strategies

In many cases the following are the barriers of HR strategies: Failure to under-stand the strategic needs of the business; in adequate assessment of the environ-mental and cultural factors that affect the content of strategies; the development of ill conceived and irrelevant initiatives due to ill digested analysis of best practice that does not fit the organization's requirements; the tendency of long term serving employees to cling to the status quo; the tendency of employees in diverse organizations only to accept initiatives they perceive to be relevant to their own areas; these problems are compounded when insufficient attention is paid to a practical implementation which should be supported by strategic capability.

People Resourcing Strategy

Many Human Resource commentators say that People Resourcing Strategy (PRS) is concerned with taking steps to ensure that the organization attracts and retains the people it needs and employs them efficiently. PRS is closely associ-ated with learning and developed strategy, which sets out how the organization ensures that it has the skilled and knowledgeable workforce it needs and that a pool of talent people is created who will provide for management succession. The concept that the strategic capability of a firm depends on its resource capability in the shape of people (resource based view) provides the rationale for resourcing strategy.

According to Armstrong (2009) the aim of this strategy is to ensure that a firm achieves competitive advantage by attracting and retaining more capable people than its rivals and employing them more effectively. Strategic HRM emphasizes the importance of human resources in achieving organizational capability and therefore the need to find people whose attitudes and behaviour are likely to be congruent with what management believes to be appropriate and conducive to success.

Additionally, strategic HRM emphasizes using a systematic approach, starting with human resource planning and proceeding through recruitment and selection, followed by performance management, learning and development, recognition and reward.

Human Resource Planning (HRP) - workforce planning

Armstrong (2009) mentions the following four human resource strategies that complement the HRP:
- Retention Strategy - preparing plans for retaining the people the organization needs. Absence management strategy - planning for the control of absence.
- Flexibility Strategy - planning for increased productivity in the use of human resources to enable the organization to make the best use of people.
- Talent Management Strategy – ensuring that the organization has the talented people it requires to provide for management succession and meet present and future business needs.
- Engagement Strategy – planning the approaches used to attract people.

The focus of Human Resource Planning (HRP) or employment planning is on the demand and supply of labour. HRP involves the acquisition, development and departure of people (employees) and it is the responsibility of all managers and not just the HR department.

The success of an organization depends on its employees. This means that its competitiveness and ultimate survival depends on having the right people in the right jobs at the right times

Human Resource Development

Strategic Human Resource Development according to Armstrong (2008) is con-cerned with the development of strategies for the provision of learning, develop-ment and training opportunities in order to improve individual, team and organ-izational performance. It is concerned with enhancing resourcing capacity in accordance with the belief that a firm's human resources are a major source of competitive advantage as well as ensuring that the right quality of people is available to meet present and future needs.

Learning a relatively permanent change in behaviour that occurs as a result of practice or experience. Education – the development of the knowledge values and understanding required in all aspects of life rather than the knowledge and skills relating to particular areas of activity.

Development – the growth or realization of a person's ability and potential through the provision of learning and educational experiences.

Training – the planned and systematic modification of behaviour through learn-ing events, programmes and instruction which enable individuals to achieve the levels of knowledge, skill and competence needed to carry out their work effec-tively.

Human Resource Development policies, strategies and practices of an organisation must be driven by the business and human resource needs of the organisation.

Performance Management

The concept has been one of the most important and positive developments in the sphere of Human Resource Management in recent years. It became recog-nized as a distinct approach in the mid-1980s. Many human resource manage-ment professionals say that performance management is a strategic and inte-grated approach to delivering sustained success to organizations by improving the performance of people who work in them and developing the capabilities of teams and individual contributors. The scope of Performance Management con-cerns the whole organization. It takes a comprehensive view of the constituents of performance, how these contribute to desired outcomes at organizational, de-partmental, team and individual levels and what needs to be done to improve these outcomes.

Performance management in its fullest sense is based on the belief that every-thing that people do at work, at any level contributes to achieve the overall pur-pose of the organization. It is therefore concerned with what people (their work), how they do it (their behaviour) and what they achieve (their results). It embraces all formal and informal measures adopted by an organization to increase corpo-rate, team and individual effectiveness and continuously to develop knowledge, skill and competence. It is not a top-down, backward looking form of appraising people. Neither is it just a method of generating information for pay decisions. It is forward looking and developmental.

Purpose of Performance Management

It is a means of getting better results from the organization, teams and individu-als by understanding and managing performance within an agreed framework of planned goals, standards and competence requirements.

Performance Management Process

It can be described as continuous self-renewing cycle consisting of the following main activities:

Issue of rewards are part of performance management.

Performance management is broader approach of managing the entire perform-ance of the organization.

Balanced Score Card

In performance management no single measure can provide a clear performance target or focus attention on the critical areas of the business. Managers want a balanced presentation of both financial and operational measures. The two there-fore devised what they called the balanced scorecard.

Essentially, the balanced scorecard is a set of measures designed to give manag-ers a fast and comprehensive view of the business. It is an attempt at looking at the overall organizational performance from four related perspectives and no one aspect dominates. Customer perspective: - How many customers see us? Internal business perspective: - what we excel at? Financial perspective: how do we look at shareholders? Innovation and learning perspective:- can we continue to improve and create value? Using a balanced scorecard can present some difficulties particularly if one measure of performance can be improved only at the expense of the other, which unfortunately is often the case.

To use the balanced scorecard approach successfully, it is vital that general statements of mission and goals be translated not just into broad corporate ob-jectives but refined through the organization into divisional departmental and individual objectives which can be measured. Further, it also requires excellent communication system throughout the organization to ensure that the measures on the scorecard are recognized, linked and understood.

360 Degrees Feedback

Multi-source assessment or multi-rater feedback) – it is a relatively new feature of performance management and is gaining increasing interest. Definition: The systematic collection and feedback of performance data on an individual or group derived from a number of the stakeholders on their performance. Thus, feedback is collected simultaneously from subordinates, peers, supervisors and supervisors and employees themselves.

Steps needed:

- Define the purpose of the 360 degree feedback
- Decide on recipients of feedback
- Decide on who will give the feedback
- Decide on the areas of work and behaviour on which feedback will be given
- Decide on the method of collecting data
- Decide on data analysis and presentation
- Plan initial implementation programme
- Analyse outcome of pilot scheme
- Plan and implement full programme
- Monitor and evaluate 360-degree feedback: criteria for success:-

- Active support to top management
- Using feedback as the basis for development
- Comprehensive and well delivered communication and training programmes
- Questionnaire items fit/reflect typical and significant aspects of behaviour
- Feedback questionnaires are relatively easy to complete.
- No one feels threatened by the process (rater confidentiality vital)

CHAPTER 14

Wealthy Thinking

Money is a concept. You can't really see or touch it. You can only do that with some physical symbol of it like bank notes or a cheque. Bits of paper yes but bits of paper with enormous power. The good news about becoming wealthy is that anybody can make money and that this is not selective or discriminatory. You have the same rights and opportunities as everyone else to take as much as you want. Of the wealth the world each has as much as they take. What else could make sense? There is no way money can know who is handling it, what qualifi-cations are, what ambitions they have or what class they belong to. It is very clear that money has no ears or eyes or senses. Money is there to be used, spent, saved and invested, fought over, se-duced with and worked for it.

Knowledge

Everything you know or believe about money did not come to you at birth. You were conditioned in your attitude towards finance as you grew in your family or environment of your up-bringing. Until the knowledge you have of finance is appropriate one for wealth creation, every plan you have gets messed up by the disjointed opinions you hold. Every time you want to create wealth you might find at the back of your mind things rising against it thus causing you make ex-cuses and reject what fi-nances are coming your way.

So thinking that money is scarce, evil, bad or dirty it will be hard for money to come to you until you get the right educa-tion. Robert Kioyosak author of Rich Dad and Poor Dad says there are three forms of education: academic, profes-sional and financial education. People are not wealthy and even go to the extent of being poor because they are financially illiterate. To be financially mis-educated is to use slow words like "I will never be rich". Financial miseducation will teach you to write strong business proposals that will create jobs for others and profit for companies and not have to create something for your future.

Multiplying money is a skill and requires that you be ad-equately informed and continue to inform yourself on how to make money and see it increase. You must ask yourself how you will put your brain to work instead of asking how you can afford things. Wealth creation rests in educating your mind and you need to know that being broke and being poor are not the same because if you are broke it is a temporary thing but pover-ty is eternal. You must educate yourself to know that multiply-ing money is necessary because money is a form of power and once you have it you have the ability to respond.

DEDICATION

Dedication and commitment is the next step after acquiring financial knowledge. Commitment must be put into action by crafting a game plan. Wealthy people would not have become who they are by chance by taking tangible actions.

If you are to leave where you are to where you ought to there must be a clear description of the map. You have got to have a plan. The plan gives you the im-portant bit – how you are going to get there. This is a function of strategic vision which is a description of the road map. This type of thinking will make you to put your heart and soul into your assignment which will create wealth for you.

Investment

Many business commentators say that investment simply means the science of money making money. This means that once your commitment towards creation is established the next thing is to start the journey in investment. This is important because you cannot become wealthy only by looking wealthy.

This is a call to develop the ability to multiplying money. With most people, when money gets into their hands, it reduces in quantity. But with some, it multiplies when it reaches their hands. Financial success and wealth is not all about spending money; it is about making money. The major problem is that most of us we were not taught how to make money in schools. Most of our money habits were picked up from our home. We learn how to spend money and not how to make money. The man with five talents traded with what he was given.

This is amazing. If you are in your 20s and 30s and you don't want to be broke at the age of 70, do something now. It is almost too late to start when you turn sixty.

Your money habits today determine your financial future. However, financial success is progressive. Until you can manage the hundreds you have, you are not prepared to handle the thousands, then millions and then billions. It is progressive. Until you pass the test on this level, God will not allow you to advance to the next level. He says:

God predicts that what you will do with the millions by what you do with the thousands. Money will always flow away from those who do not know how to treat it well to those who know how to treat it well. Different ways to invest in-clude leveraging, treasury bills, investing in stocks, bonds, general business, mutual trust funds, real estate and investing in financial institu-tions such as banks.

That is the minimum, the least. Here we cannot talk about the savings account. The interest you earn from the savings ac-count is not multiplication. It is a re-duction of your money. By the time you factor in inflation at the end of one year and add interest on it, you will realize that the rate of inflation is higher than the interest your money is earning hence you would have lost money in real terms. From today you will not be on the los-ing end but prospering side.

How to be Wealthy

Riches require that you have enough money. But wealth goes further. It is having enough of all the essential of life such as love, good health, friends and family, spiritually and of course, enough money. What we are saying is that being wealthy is a to-tal package – laughter, love, living, good health, peace, money and relationships.

The following are proven ways on how you can become wealthy: wealthy think-ing; developing an understanding of the power of small and big savings; spending less than you earn; always paying yourself first; saving something out of each dollar; being responsible for where you are in life; paying cash and use less credit; buy stocks not product; keeping track of your mon-ey; study and admire the successful in your chosen assignment or field; recognize the difference between income statement wealth and balance sheet wealth; do not confuse between debt and wealth; invest in right ground; form new habits which encourage you in the direction of becoming wealthy for God; set fi-nancial goals and assess them; refuse to be stressed; make con-scious decision to handle your money matters yourself; create your own entity; become financially literate and give generously.

How to Stay Wealthy

To maintain or sustain wealth is a skill and it requires com-mitment to the proven wealth principles. It is a matter of fol-lowing the rules of the game. It goes without saying that those that love rules will be rulers and those that love commandments will be in command.

To stay wealth requires you to follow certain rules. Here are the rules: don't spend it before you've got it; put something aside for your old age – no more than that; put something aside for emergencies or rainy days – this the contingency fund; never borrow money from friends or family but you can allow them to invest; don't surrender equity; know when to stop; never lend money to a friend unless you are prepared to write off; find ways to give people money without them feeling they are in your debt and lastly share your wealth.

Sharing wealth simply means using wealth wisely. Those who abuse their wealth don't tend to stay wealth for long. Sharing wealthy is the same as giving. We are not to be mere reservoirs that hold on to the blessing, but those who will pass it for others too to enjoy. When God called Abraham, He said He would bless him to be a blessing to his generation. The process of giving and receiving is what makes the cycle of life to be perpetuated and be enjoyable. Those that keep to themselves do not increase. There is that scatterth and yet increaseth and there is that with holdeth more than is meet but it tendereth to poverty.

PART IV

Creation of Wealth Through
Entrepreneurship

CHAPTER 15

The Importance of Entrepreneurs to Wealth Creation

THE SYSTEM OF ENTREPRENEURSHIP is supposed to foster the spirit of entrepreneurship. In fact, the future of such countries is independent on entrepreneurs and become the economic power due to entrepreneurial activity. The future of any nation will be greatly influenced by entrepreneurs with their unique and innovative ideas. Thus entrepreneurs are motivated and inspired individuals willing to accept risk and seize opportunities to harness and use resources in novel ways.

How to Become and Stay Wealthy

It goes without saying that we all want to do better by staying wealthy, rich and abundant. And we are fascinated as well as envying those who already are. The question is how did they do it? What magic did they use? How can we do it too? The simple truth is that wealthy people tend to understand and do things the rest of us do not. From mind-sets to casual actions, they follow behavioural rules when it comes to their wealth and these rules are what separate them from everybody else. This chapter codifies what those behaviours are so that you too can choose to be more wealthy. The basis of the rules is that these are the things I have observed wealthy people do. This means that if we do like them, we will become like them. This actually does work.

Wealth creation involves knowing what to do to make money, how to carry on making money, how to hang on it once you have got, how to spend, invest and enjoy money and make use of it altruistically. This assumes that you want to get richer, do it legally, do something useful with it once you have got it, put some-thing back, keep some of this stuff under your hat and that you are prepared to put a bit of work.

Therefore this chapter is about thinking wealth, getting wealth, staying wealthy

The entrepreneur is the catalysis that brings together the resources of land, labour, and capital to create valuable goods and services and in the hopes of build-ing a profitable business. As stated earlier the word entrepreneur is of French origin and derives from entreprendre, which means 'to undertake.' The American heritage dictionary defines an entrepreneur as "a person who organizes, operates, and assumes the risk for a business venture.

The entrepreneur plays a vital role in society. Without entrepreneurs, there would be no businesses, no inventions, no innovations, no progress, and no wealth. Without the entrepreneur and the system that provides incentives for entrepreneurs, we would have no printing press, no bifocals, no airplane, no air conditioner, no radio, no micro wave, no computer, no telephone, no television, and no George Foreman Lean Mean Fat Burning Grilling Machine.

In short, the standard of living would not be much better than that of 1450. The world would not be able to support the 6.5 billion person it does, and the dooms-day Malthusian predictions of overpopulation would have been realized many decades, if not centuries ago.

Entrepreneurs develop new markets. Under the modern concept of marketing, markets are people who are willing and able to satisfy their needs. In economics, this is called effective demand. Entrepreneurs are different from ordinary busi-nessmen who only perfume traditional functions of management like planning organization, and coordination.

According to Peters (2008) entrepreneurs discover new sources of materials. This means that entrepreneurs are never satisfied with traditional or existing sources of materials to improve their enterprise in terms of supply, cost and quality.

Nellis (2007) says that entrepreneurs mobilize capital resources. David (2010) concurs with Nellis (2012) views by mentioning that entrepreneurs are the organ-izers and coordinators of the major factors of production, such as land, labour and capital. This means that they properly mix these factors of production to cre-ate goods and service.

Lash (2010) argues that capital resources, from a layman's view, refer to money.

However, these views are counter argued by Gerson (2008) who states that capital resources represent machine, buildings and other physical production resources. Therefore, entrepreneurs have initiatives and self-confidence in accumulating and mobilization capital resources for new business or business expansions. Entrepreneurs introduce new technologies, new industries and new products. Aside from being innovators and reasonable takers, entrepreneurs take advantage of business opportunities, and transform these into profits. They introduce something new or something different. Such entrepreneurial spirit has greatly contributed to the modernization of the economy. Every year, there are new technologies and new products. All of these are intended to satisfy human needs in more convenient and pleasant way.

Entrepreneurs create employment. Factories, services industries, agricultural enterprise, and the numerous small- scale business provide millions of jobs. Such massive employment has multiplier and accelerator in the whole economy. More jobs means more income. This increases demand for goods and services. In addition, this stimulates production. Again, more production requires more employment.

Have you ever wondered why some countries are relatively wealthy and others poor? Economists have been studying the issue of wealth creation for many years. They began the process by staying potential sources of wealth to deter-mine which are the most important. Overtime they came up with five factors that seemed to contribute to wealth. They called them factors of production. These are

- Land (natural resources)
- labour (workers)
- Capital (this includes machines, tools, buildings or whatever else is used in production of goods. It does not include money; money is used to buy factors of production – it is not a factor itself.)
- Entrepreneurship
- Knowledge

Traditionally, business and economic textbooks have emphasized only four fac-tors of production: land, labour, capital and entrepreneurship.

But management expert and business consultant Peter Drucker says that the important factor of production is and always will be knowledge.

If you were to analyse rich countries versus poor countries to see what causes the differences in the levels of wealth, you would have to look at the factors of production in each country. Such analyses have revealed that some relatively poor countries often have plenty of land and natural resources. Most poor coun-tries have many labourers, so it's not labour that is the primary source of wealth today. Labourers need to find work to make a contribution; that is, they need entrepreneurs to provide jobs for them. Further more capital – machinery and tools – is now becoming available in world markets, so capital isn't the missing ingredient. Capital is not productive without entrepreneurs to put into use.

Clearly, then what makes rich countries rich today is a contribution of entrepreneurship and the effective use of knowledge. Together, lack of entrepreneurship and the absence of knowledge among workers, along with the lack of freedom, contribute to keeping poor countries poor. The box called Reaching Beyond Our Borders discusses the importance of freedom to economic development.

Entrepreneurship also makes some countries rich while others remain relatively poor. The business environment either encourages or discourages entrepreneur-ship. In the following chapter, we will explore what makes up the business environment and how to build an environment that encourages growth and job creation.

Why Individual Productivity is Key to Successful Free Market Economy

When many folks hear the phrase "wealth of Nations," they immediately think of Adam Smith's legendary social economic work published in 1776 under the full title of An Inquiry into the Nature and Causes of Wealth of Nations. The work was one of the first serious thought pieces regarding how wealth is created and the role of market based economic concepts, such as division of labour, productivity and the usefulness of free markets.

At times the world's leaders have attacked the usefulness of free-market economic systems, declaring market – based systems uncaring and inhuman. While some would argue the truth of these sentiments, free – market economies have lifted up the vast majority of Western

Societies to levels of prosperity that were only dreams as little as 150 years ago. However, simply claiming an economic system to be market based rather than command – based isn't enough to promote high levels of growth. A focus on productivity is needed for strong sustainable growth to occur and for society as a whole to prosper.

The difference between Income and Wealth

Many economic and business commentators on one hand say that income is a flow of money that goes into factors of production. This include: Wages and salaries paid to people from their jobs; money paid to people receiving welfare benefits such as pension; profits flowing to people who own and lease property; rental income flowing to people who own and lease out property and interest paid to those who hold money in deposit accounts or who own bonds. On the other hand economic and business commentators say that wealth is a stock concept. It is a large amount of money or valuable possessions and can be held in different ways: savings held in bank deposits; ownership of shares issued by listed companies and equity stakes in private businesses; the ownership of property; wealth held in bonds and wealth held in occupational pension schemes and life assurance schemes. Wealth generates income for if you have built up savings balances they aught to pay interest.

M any Dimensions of Poverty

A plethora of definitions of poverty has emerged. Poverty is hunger. Poverty is lack of shelter. Poverty is being sick and not being able to see a doctor. Poverty is not having access to school and not knowing how to read. Poverty is not having a job and is fear for the future, living one day at a time. Poverty is powerlessness, lack of representation and freedom. The prosperity of each individual constitutes the wealth of the nation which eventually help to finance the public sector.

Inequality in the distribution of income and wealth

Living standards depend on the level of economic activity and on the redistribution of resources within society as a whole. The level of inequality of income and wealth can be measured by:

The share of national income going to different groups in society, the poorest 20% of households at the bottom of the income scale through to the richest 20 %.

The proportion of all households who must live on an income below an official 'poverty line.'

The New System to Wealth of a Nation

If the countries are to enjoy wealth the new system that measures the wealth of nations must be developed. The system must integrate economic, social and environmental factors. This could be a major addition to the international perspectives that have looked only at income and is the first time that wealth will be calculated to nearly all countries of the world. The new system could challenge thinking by looking at wealth and not just income in determining growth strategies of countries. It also expands the concept of wealth beyond money and in-vestments.

The new system to wealth of nations bases the real wealth of nations on a combination of:

- Natural Capital – The economic value of land and water among others
- Produced Assets – Machinery, factories, infrastructure: water systems, roads, railways etc.
- Human Resources – value represented by people's productive capacity
- Social Capital – The productive value of human organizations and institutions such as families and communities not represented in the individual but in the collective processes.

From the foregoing many people look for causes of poor economic performance primarily in macroeconomics. An evaluation of economic performance requires an analysis at the level of individual and business levels. However, beyond mac-roeconomic policies, economic analysis usually ends up attributing most of the differences in economic performance to differences in labour and capital mar-kets. This conclusion is inccorrect. Differences in competition in product markets are much more important. Policies governing competition in the product market are as important as macroeconomic policies.

Many people see access to capital as the determining factor between a productive growing economy and one that is not. Therefore they feel that if rich countries
sent capital pouring into poor countries, the poor countries would become richer. The solution does not start with more capital. The solution, rather is in the coun-try's productivity or the way it organizes and deploys both its labour and its capital. If poor countries improved productivity and balanced their budgets, they would have plenty of capital for growth from domestic and savers and foreign investors.

Most people consider "social objectives to be good. Import tariffs, subsidized loans for businesses, government disallowance of layoffs and high minimum wages are all examples of economic policies designed to achieve social objectives. We can not have both ways. These measures distort markets severely and limit productivity growth, slow overall economic growth and cause unemploy-ment. Rather than support these measures, it is better to level the the playing field, create bigger economic pie and manage the distribution of that pie through tax code for individuals.

Some people don't recognize the destructive power of the government on eco-nomic development. Big governments demand taxation. When part of the economy is informal and untaxed the burden falls heavily on legitimate businesses. This is a burden in today's rich countries did not have when they were poor. Additionally, many think that production is all that is needed to create economic value. This is why government sometimes protects businesses, regardless of their performance. They fail to make the link between production and consumption. The goods produced have value only because consumers want them. If they do not want them for some reason the business producing them needs to die. Only one force can stand up to producer special interests – consumer interests. Most poor countries are a long way from consumption mind set and consumer rights. As a result they are poor.

Other people in an economy think that nations should protect their own indus-tries but also ask outside nations for capital. This is wrong. Direct investment by the more productive companies from the rich countries would raise the poor countries' productivity and growth rates far more effectively than sending them money. Poor countries have the potential to grow much faster than most people realize.

PART V

Managing Within the
Dynamic and Complex
Environment: Taking Risks
and Making Profits

CHAPTER 16

The Business Environment

Environmental Analysis

ONE ESSENTIAL ROLE OF an entrepreneurial management is strategy formulation. Before an organisation can begin strategy formulation, it must scan the external environment to identify possible opportunities and threats and internal environment for strength and weaknesses. Environmental analysis (scanning) is therefore the process of monitoring an organization's environment to identify strengths, weaknesses, opportunities and threats (SWOT factors) that may influence the firm's ability to reach its goals. The environmental scanning generally focuses on identifying present and future strategic issues and planning how to effectively deal with them.

Basic Structure of Environment

There are three distinct levels that form the basic structure of a business environ-ment. These are the general (or societal) environment, the operating (or task) environment and the internal environment.

The General Environment

The general environment consists of the surrounding factors that either help or hinder the development of businesses. There are five elements in the general en-vironment. These are:
- The economic and legal environment
- The technological environment
- The competitive environment

- The social environment
- The global business environment

Businesses grow and prosper in a health environment. The results are job growth and wealth that makes it possible to have both a high standard of living and a high quality of life. The wrong environmental conditions, in contrast, lead to business failure, loss of jobs and standard of living and quality of life, In short creating the right business environment is the foundation for social progress of all kinds, including good schools, clean air and water, good health care and low rates of crime.

The Economic and Legal Environment

People are willing to start new businesses if they believe that the risk of losing their money isn't too great. Part of the risk involves the economic system and how government works with or against businesses. Government can do a lot to lessen the risk of starting businesses and thus increase entrepreneurship and wealth. For example, a government can keep taxes and regulations to a minimum.

Entrepreneurs are looking for high return on investment (ROI), including the investment of their time. If the government takes away much of what a business earns through high taxes, the ROI may no longer be worth the risk. This is true even within wealthy countries like United States. Countries that have high taxes and restrictive regulations tend to drive entrepreneurs out while countries with low taxes and less restrictive regulations attract entrepreneurs. Laws that encourage entrepreneurship have been enacted all across the world. Some of the tax laws that help businesses include the provisions for deducting home office expenses, business travel and meals and other business expenses.

One way for government to actively promote entrepreneurship is to allow private ownership of businesses. In some countries the government owns most businesses and thus there is little incentive for people to work hard or create profit. All around the world today, however, various countries in which the government formerly owned most businesses are selling those businesses to private individuals to create wealth through privatization process. Privatization is the transfer or sell of government assets to the private sector or individuals.

The Technological Environment

Computers, Modems, Cellular Phones. Chief among these is the internet. Although many internet firms have failed in recent years, the Internet will prove to be a major force in business in the coming years.

How technology benefits workers and you. One of the advantages of working for others is that the company often provides the tools and technology to make your job more productive. Technology means everything from phones and copiers to computers, medical imaging devices, personal digital assistants and various software programmes that make business processes more efficient resources. Productivity is the amount of output you generate given the amount of input. The ratio of productivity (Output/Input) must be greater than 1.

The Competitive Environment

The competition among businesses has never been greater than it is today. Some companies have found a competitive edge by focusing on quality. The goals for many companies is zero defects – no mistakes in making the product. However, simply making a high quality product is not enough to allow a company to stay competitive in world markets. Companies now have to offer both high-quality products and outstanding service at competitive prices (value) with speed advantage. Manufacturers and service organizations throughout the world have learned that today's customers are very demanding. Not only do they want good quality at low prices, but they want great service as well. In fact, some products in the 21st century will be designed to facilitate, bewitch and delight customers, exceeding and even amazing their customers. Business is becoming customer-driven not management driven as in the past. This means that customers' wants and needs must come first. Successful organizations must now listen more closely to customers to determine their wants and needs, and then adjust the firm's products, policies, and practices to meet those demands.

Social Environment

The social environment, social context, social cultural context or milieu refers to the immediate physical and social setting in which people live or in which some-thing happens or develops. It includes the culture that the individual was educated or lives in, and the people and institutions with whom they interact.

The interaction may be in person or through communication media, even anonymous or one-way, and may not imply equality of social status. Therefore, the social environment is a broader concept than that of social class or social circle.

The Global Environment

The global environment of business is so important that we show it as surrounding all other environmental influences. Two important environmental changes in recent years have been the growth of international competition and the increase of free trade among nations. Japanese manufacturers like Honda, Mitsubishi and Sony won much of the market for automobiles and other products by offering good consumers products of higher quality than those made by U.S. manufactur-ers. This competition hurt many U.S. industries and many jobs were lost. Re-cently, U.S. businesses have become more competitive and Japan's economy is now suffering. Today, manufacturers in countries such as China, India, South Korea and Mexico can produce high – quality goods at low prices because their workers are paid less money than U.S. workers and because they have learned quality concepts from Japanese, German and U.S. producers.

The Operating (Task) Environment

The task environment has components that normally have relatively specific and immediate implications for managing an organization. These components include supplier component, customers component, competitive component, labour component and international component.

Some businesses have value statements that state "customer is the reason we exist" Basically, customers purchase and consume an organization's goods and services. Providing customers with what they want, how, when and where they want it is fundamental to organization's success. The ways to achieve this are to provide quality products and prompt customer service. Exploring and studying consumers' buying patterns and habits can be pertinent to easily target their needs and discover if at all the existing products meet those needs or if a new good or service could find a niche.

Considering competition is another important aspect entrepreneurs need to con-sider seriously. The competitive environment includes such factors such as how the firm or business rates in the market share, technological innovation, financial strength, involvement in growth industries and the development of its human resources.

A business might be financially sound have good human resource and dominate its industry, yet if the business is positioned in a declining industry, an entrepre-neur or management may have to take aggressive action to move it to new ex-panding markets. One important point to note is that competitive environment is not static, instead it is dynamic.

The importance of other components of the operating environment need not be emphasized. For instance suppliers provide raw materials, goods or services require by an organization in order to function. Suppliers can therefore help or hurt, build or break an organization or business depending on their ability to provide needed materials at the right time. On its part the supply of labour has a lot of bearing on the success of an organization or business. Availability of qual-ity and skilled labour tends to determine the past, present and future shape of a firm.

The Internal Environment

This has forces that operate in the business with specific implications for manag-ing business performance. It involves the organizational component, marketing component, financial component, production component and personal component (values, heroes, rites and other cultural networks). This basically tends to focus on how the business is going to perform as an entity.

CHAPTER 17

Business and Entrepreneurship

AS INDICATED IN EARLIER chapters one of the ways to become a suc-cess is to start a business. A business is any activity that seeks to provide goods and services to others while operating at a profit. Profit is the amount of money a business earns above and beyond what it spends. In simple terms profit can be defined as revenue above costs. Since not all businesses make a profit starting a business can be a risky proposition. As said earlier an entrepreneur is a person who risks time and money to start and manage a business. Once an entrepreneur has started a business there is usually a need for good managers and other workers to keep the business going. However, not all entrepreneurs are skilled at being managers. Business provide people with opportunity to become wealthy.

Matching Risk with Profit

Profit remember is the amount of money a business earns above and beyond what it pays out for salaries and other expenses. Revenue is the total amount of money a business takes during a given period by selling goods and services. A loss occurs when a business's expenses are more than its revenue. If a business loses money over time it will likely have to close and this will put its employees out of work. Therefore starting business involves risk. Risk is a chance an entrepreneur takes of losing time and money on a business that may not prove profitable. Even companies that do make profit not all companies make the same amount. Those companies that take high risk make the most profit. There is a saying that goes, "the higher the risk the higher the returns."

As a business owner you need to do research to find the right balance between risk and profit for you.

Business Add to the Standard of Living and Quality of Life

Entrepreneurs such as Bill Gates (Microsoft) not only become wealthy them-selves by starting successful businesses; they also provide employment for other people. Employees pay taxes which government uses to finance the public sector. Businesses too, pay taxes to government and that money can be used to build schools, hospitals and other such facilities. Thus the wealth businesses generate revenue and taxes they pay help every one in their communities. A nation's busi-nesses are part of an economic system that contributes to the standard of living and quality of life for everyone in the country.

The term standard of living refers to the amount of goods and services people can buy with their money. However, the cost of goods differs from country to coun-try. The reasons why goods cost more in one country and less in the other include high taxes and stricter government regulations. Funding the right level of taxes and regulation is an important step towards making a country prosperous.

The term quality of life refers to the general well-being of society in terms of political freedom, a clean natural environment, education, health care, safety, free time and everything else that leads to satisfaction and joy. Maintaining a high quality of life requires the combined efforts of businesses, non - profit organizations and government agencies. The more money businesses create, the more is potentially available to improve the quality of life for everyone.

Entrepreneurship Versus Working for Others

There are two ways to succeed in business. One way is to rise up through the ranks of large corporations. The advantage of working for others is that someone else assumes the entrepreneurial risk and provides you with benefits such as paid vacation time and health insurance. Most people choose that option. It is a very good option and can lead to a happy prosperous life. Businesses need good man-agers to succeed and all workers contribute to producing and marketing the goods and services that increase the quality of life and standard of living for others.

The other more risky part is to start your own business. Thus, it takes a brave person to start a business. Further, more as an entrepreneur you do not receive any benefits such as paid vacation and health insurance. You have to provide them for yourself.

Business investment vs personal wealth creation

Wealth creation paths require careful planning, commitment and on-going atten-tion. For many, the sole focus is to invest all their energies and cash into the business, so that it strengthens and grows and secures its longevity for future generations. While admirable and effective, it may not always be the most ap-propriate strategy to adopt.

The key is to be conscious that building wealth should not always be through one medium – the business – and you need to plan and be proactive in building your overall personal wealth. With this in mind, what are the considerations?

The purpose of business leadership is to create wealth – financial and material, human and social – in the face of external developments that are never entirely foreseeable. The CEO must create a CXO team (CXOs are the chiefs of business functions and units) that can successfully carry out this wealth-creating mission. With this in mind, we have explored the tasks that comprise purposeful contribu-tion by members of the top executive team, the CXOs. In doing so, we have ex-amined key business imperatives, and the work of the CXOs and the CEO.

Building capability for wealth creation

The fundamental business imperatives in business leadership are the capabilities, methods and mind-sets that all entrepreneurs must develop to help the firm re-spond effectively to challenges of today and tomorrow. Nurturing and managing talented people, learning from experience and instilling the ethos of quality-mindedness are particularly important here.

Talent

Entrepreneurs must create and manage large pools of managers and other profes-sionals who can devise methods to capitalize on opportunities, and overcome threatening challenges. To develop talent, an entrepreneur should expose these people to stretching experiences. This helps them recognize things from emergent perspectives and not just from their earlier learned beliefs.

More generally, senior executives must find and promote people who can deal well with conflict because changes in external circumstances and uncertainty about what these changes will lead to, inevitably generates disagreement among those involved.

Entrepreneurs must also set up systems to detect emerging signals about key de-velopments in the firm's business system: for example, in customer concerns or product quality. Then they must ensure that both confirming and distressing in-formation is appropriately amplified and transmitted to the people who must re-act to the concerns.

Entrepreneurs must follow through on decisions for improvements; first, by find-ing creative ways for testing out ideas on a small scale before committing major resources in an irreversible way; and second, by adjusting the surrounding sys-tems – that is, structure and processes – to fit in with and support the new prac-tices.

Leading within the function

Entrepreneurs must lead within their function or business area which typically requires finding the right mix of three arenas of purposeful activity: 1) managing current operations; 2) preparing for change, and implementing projects that ac-complish the required transitions; and 3) ensuring that these two remain in har-mony with, and contribute to, the overall company strategy.

Teamwork, yes: But individuals make the difference The entrepreneur's task is to devise a highly robust management system comprising the necessary mission, structure, processes and culture, staffed by talented people, to accomplish the business objectives, whatever difficulties might arise. In highly effective executive teams, wealth creation is the result when each member diagnoses, either alone or with colleagues, and subsequently makes his or her best possible personal contribution. Magical team-level creativity is very rare; it simply does not occur without high-quality, high-contributing individual members. Entrepreneurs must be the role models of wealth-creating behaviour for all members of the company, by showing individual leadership and by demonstrating teamwork.

PART VI

The Legal Environment
of Business

CHAPTER 18

Business Law

Law of Contract

What Contract is all about?

CONTRACT IS AN agreement between two or more parties that creates obligation on them that law will recognize and enforce. The enforceability of the agreement arises from the moral premise that an individual who voluntarily assumes an obligation that creates expectations in others should fulfil that obligation. However, all contracts are agreements but not all agreements are contracts; Thus, for there to be a valid contract, there must be at least the follow-ing five (5) essentials:

Essentials of a Valid Contract:
Agreement

An agreement which is enforceable as a contract may be oral or in writing. This is because there is generally no legal requirements that an agreement should be in writing for it to be treated by law as a legally binding contract. As a result an agreement will be enforced by law as a contract even though it is not in writing at all. In fact the largest number of contracts are never in writing. They are oral. The method which the courts determine whether an agreement has been reached is to enquire whether one party has made an offer which the other party has accepted. As stated earlier for most types of contract the offer and acceptance may be made orally in writing or they may be implied from the conduct of the parties.

Offer

An offer can be described as an expression of willingness by one person (the offeror) to enter into a contract with another person (the offeree) made with an intention that it should be binding on the offeror as soon as it is accepted by the offeree. Thus, if for example, A goes into a shop picks up a bottle of coke and walks to paying counter with money in his hands which he puts on the counter, that will be an offer to buy the drink. Consequently if the shop attendant accepts the money in payment for the coke, a contract will have been concluded between him and the shop for the sale of the Coke.

Invitation to Offers

However it should be noted that not every apparent offer will be regarded as such by law. Some words or conduct which may appear to be offers are not offers at all. For example, an advertisement of goods for sale is not an offer of the goods for sale. Similarly the display of goods in a shop window or on a shop shelf is also not an offer of the goods for sale.

Termination of an Offer

An offer will not constitute an agreement unless it is accepted before it is termi-nated by the offeror. As a result where the offeree purports to accept an offer that has already been terminated, his/her acceptance will not be valid to convert the offer into an agreement between him and the offeror. An offer can be termi-nated through the following ways:
- Counter Offer
- Revocation
- Rejection
- Lapse of Time
- Un occurrence of an event

Acceptance

An offer cannot constitute an agreement unless it is first accepted by the offeree. In other words, it is the combination of an offer and acceptance that creates an agreement which will be enforced as a contract. Under the law of contract, an acceptance is defined as a final and unqualified expression of assent to the terms of an offer.

Communication of Acceptance

Generally, an acceptance must be communicated to the offeror so that in the absence of that, there will be no contract. In other words the acceptance must be brought to the offeror's notice. Accordingly there is no contract where the offeree writes his acceptance of the offer on a piece of paper which he keeps himself.

Consideration

Although there may be a valid agreement constituted by an offer which is ac-cepted, the agreement may not be enforced as a contract in the absence of 'consideration'. Consideration shall mean something of value in the eyes of law.

The basis of this rule is the fact that courts are not willing to enforce gratuitous promises as contracts. For this purpose, consideration is either some benefit to the offeror or some detriment to the offeree. Thus payment by the buyer is con-sideration for the seller's delivery. Conversely, delivery or promise of delivery by the seller is consideration for the buyer's payment or promise of payment. This can be described either as a detriment to the seller or as a benefit to the buyer.

In law of contract past consideration is no consideration at all. For this reason, payment for past services is generally not contractually binding as valid consid-eration unless the services were rendered on the premise that the payment would be made at some future date.

Privity of Contract

Because of the importance of consideration in the enforcement of a contract, generally only parties to a contract will be allowed to enforce it In other words, a person who is not a party to contract (i.e. who has not provided consideration) will not be allowed to enforce the contract even if it was concluded for his benefit. For example if a father enters into a contract to buy a car for his son and the seller refuses to deliver the vehicle after payment for it has been made, the son cannot sue the seller for the delivery of the car. Only the father who has given consideration for the sale has that right.

Terms of Contract

When one party to a contract brings a court action against the other party it is often on the ground that the latter has failed to fulfil his obligation under the con-tract. Now whether a party to a contract is under any contractual obligation de-pends on whether performance of that obligation is part of, or a term of, the con-tract.

1. EXPRESS

A term of contract is express if it is orally agreed upon by the parties at the time of concluding the contract or is contained in a written document embodying the contract.

2. IMPLIED

A term may also be implied. It will be implied by conduct where even though they may not specifically have discussed it or agreed on it, they should, as rea-sonable people be taken to have intended that it should be part of the contract. For example in a contract of employment, whether the parties specifically agreed on it or not, it will be implied that the employee should be paid his salary in full in any month if he is absent from work without permission or reasonable cause. Similarly, if it is customary in any industry that employees should receive a bo-nus at a certain point in time, that will be a term implied into their contracts of employment.

Lastly, law implies a number of terms into specific contracts. For instance, it is an implied term in a contract for the sale of goods that the goods should be fit for their intended use. Again, it is an implied term of a contract of employment that the employee should be entitled to a certain number of days every year as his annual leave

Conditions and Warranties

A term of contract (whether express or implied) may be a condition of the contract or a mere warranty Although whether it is one or the other may depend on how it is called by the parties in their agreement, often that is not enough. Generally a condition is such an important term of contract that its breach by one party deprives the other of a substantial benefit of the contract so that he is entitled, if he so wishes, to regard himself as discharged from further performance of the contract. On the other hand a warranty is a minor term so that its breach does not entitle the innocent party to consider himself discharged from further performance of the contract

Discharge of a Contract

A party to a contract may be discharged (i.e., released) from further performance of the contract by the following factors.

Mutual Agreement

This will happen where, after their agreement, they enter into a subsequent agree-ment whereby one of the parties is released from his/her obligations under the contract. After the conclusion of that subsequent agreement, the party released will be discharged from further performance of the contract

Performance

A party to a contract may also be discharged by performance. For instance, where a contract is for the performance of specific tasks, once the party concerned completes that task, he has no further performance to render and the contract will automatically come to an end

Breach

As observed above, a breach by one party of a condition of the contract entitles the other party to regard himself as discharged from further performance of the contract. As a result the latter can terminate the contract and proceed to recover any payment he may have made or any benefit he was supposed to get under the contract

Frustration

A party to a contract may also be discharged from further performance by frus-tration. This type of discharge occurs where a contract that was capable of per-formance at the time of its conclusion becomes incapable of performance be-cause of subsequent developments.

These developments may be:
- subsequent illegality
- subsequent death of one of the parties
- Subsequent imprisonment of one of the parties for a substantial period of time and
- Subsequent cancellation of an expected event

The effect of these developments will be to bring the contract to an end forth-with and

Remedies

Where the court is satisfied that there has been a breach of contract, it has the power to grant the following remedies: i. Refusal of further performance by the innocent party. For example, if he has not yet paid the contract price, he can refuse to do so as a result of the party's breach; ii. Damages as compensation for injury or loss suffered by the innocent party as a result of the breach; iii. Quan-tum meruit, i.e. the value of the performance actually rendered by the innocent party; iv. Specific performance. This remedy allows the innocent party to recover the performance promised by the party in breach and is generally not available except in cases involving land. Thus, for instance on a breach of the contract for the sale of goods, the court will rarely order the seller to deliver the goods agreed to be sold unless they are unique in some way. Usually in that case it will simply award the innocent party damages representing the value of the good. On the other hand where a seller of land fails or refuses to transfer the land to the buyer, the court will order the seller to effect the transfer. iv. Injunction; this is an order by the court stopping a contemplated or continuing breach of contract. Of course this remedy is not final but interim. As a result it is not uncommon to have an injunction vacated by the court on the application of the party against whom it is granted. Besides an injunction often tends to be for a fixed period of time and will lapse at the expiry of that period unless the court agrees to its extension.

Law of Agency

This is the relation which exists between two persons where one of them has authority or capacity to act on behalf of the other. In other words, agency rela-tion arises whenever one person called the 'agent' has authority to create legal obligations between the other called the 'principal' and third parties. Thus, an agent is only an intermediary between the other called the 'principal' and third parties. As a result although he is bound to exercise his authority in accordance with all the lawful instructions of his principal, an agent is not (unless he is also an employee of his principal) subject to the direct control or supervision of his principal in the performance of his duties.

Creation of the Agency Relation

The agency relation may be created by the express or implied agreement (which may be but does not need to be contractual) of the principal and the agent.

1. Express Agency

Express agency arises where the principal or some person authorized by him ex-pressly (i.e. in writing or orally) appoints the agent to do either a specified num-ber of things or to act for the principal generally.

2. Implied Agency

On the other hand implied agency will arise from the conduct or situation of the parties. And it is immaterial for this purpose that the third person had no author-ity in fact at the time to enter into that contract for the first person. This is called the doctrine of apparent authority or agency by estoppels.

3. Agency by Ratification

Under some circumstances an act which at the time when it was done lacked au-thority may by the subsequent conduct of the person on whose behalf lacked au-thority. For instance, if one person acts in such a way as to lead another person into believing that he has authorized a third person to act on his behalf and that other person in that belief enters into a contract with the third person. The third person will be an agent for the first person in respect of that contract. This is be-cause the first person is prevented from denying the fact that the person had no authority in fact the third person is his agent. Every act that is not void can be ratified so long as it is capable of ratification by the principal. The illegality of an act does not of itself prevent its ratification. Consequently, a principal may ratify a breach of contract and thus become liable for it

Ratification may be express or may be inferred in appropriate cases even from silence or mere acquiescence. Of course in that latter case it must be based on the principal's full knowledge of all the essential facts of the act sought to be ratified and must relate to that particular act, and not some other transaction. As a result the agent will be relieved of personal liability to his principal for acting in excess of his authority and to the third party for possible breach of warrant of authority.

Elements to be present in ratification

(a) The agent must not have been acting for himself in the first place but must have professed to be acting on behalf of a named or ascertainable principal

(b) The principal must have been in existence at the time of the action

This is because a principal who was not in existence at the time when an act was purportedly done on his behalf cannot, on coming into existence, ratify the act

(c) The principal must have been capable of doing the act himself since a person cannot act as an agent for another person who has no capacity to act for himself

(d) The ratification must take place within the time fixed by the transaction itself or within a reasonable time thereafter

4. Agency by Necessity

The agency relation may also arise by necessity. This will be the case where by reason of an emergency, the relation of principal and agent is deemed to exist between persons who are not other wise in such a relation. Agency of necessity exists between persons who are not otherwise in such a relation. An agency of necessity exists where to prevent destruction of perishable cargo, a carrier has to take prompt action in excess of his authority and dispose of it.

In other words, as a result of the emergency the agent has to extend his authority to save the principal's property from destruction. For an agency of necessity to arise:

- The agent should not have been able to communicate with his principal on how to deal with the emergency
- The action taken should have been necessary in the circumstance in that it was the only reasonable and prudent course open to the agent; and
- The agent should have acted bona fide in the interests of the parties concerned
- Acting in Principle's name
- But regardless of the type of authority involved since an agent derives his authority from his principal, he must act in the principal's name However, as will be shown below the requirement is simply that he must disclose the principal's existence though he may not divulge the principal's identity

Agent's Capacity to Delegate

An agent cannot delegate his authority except with the principal's express or im-plied assent

As a result in the absence of that assent, the principal will not be bound by the act or contract of a sub-agent whose appointment he has not sanctioned

Sale of Goods

Contract of Sale of Goods

This is defined as a contract whereby one person (the seller) transfers or agrees to transfer the property in goods to another person (the buyer) for a money consid-eration called the price. Thus from this definition it will be clear that the legal objective of the contract of sale of goods is for the buyer to obtain ownership of the goods while the seller receives their price in exchange.

The definition excludes any transaction intended to operate by way of mortgage, pledge, charge or other security. It does not apply to bailment, barter, contract of hire, hire-purchase and contracts for labour and materials. From the statutory definition, it is clear that the following elements must exist in a contract for it to amount to a contract of sale of goods

Buyer and Seller

The buyer is defined as a person who buys or agrees to sell goods. In other words agreement is not a contract for the sale of goods unless the buyer is bound to buy the goods and the seller is to sell them to him. As a result where there is a mere option to buy them 9as under the hire purchase) there will be no account for the sale of goods

Money Consideration

As definition of a contact of sale of goods it is clear that only contracts under which property in goods is transferred for money will be considered contracts for the sale of goods. On the other hand, a part –exchange transaction in which the agreed price s payable partly in money and

Goods.

"Goods" refer to all movable property that is capable of transfer from one person to another by delivery.

For the purposes of the contract of sale of goods, goods may be specific, ear marked (i.e. identified by the parties at the time of making the contract) and or unascertained, that is unidentified at the time of the contract and therefore re-quiring some subsequent agreed act of appropriation by the buyer or seller to earmark them to the contract

Property in Goods

As noted by definition, a contract for sale of goods involves the transfer of property in goods from the seller to the buyer. For this purpose it would seem that the word "property" refers to the seller's absolute title to goods so that for a person to be able to sell goods under the contract of sale of goods, he must have a right of dominion over them

Form

There is no legal formalities required for the conclusion of a valid sale of goods

Passing of Property

When goods are transferred the risk of loss or damage to the goods also passes from the seller to the buyer with the transfer of property

Again in the event of the seller becoming bankrupt or going into liquidation with-out having delivered specific goods, the buyer's right to claim possession of the goods from the seller's trustee in bankruptcy or liquidator will depend on whether property in the goods passed to the buyer before the commencement of the bankruptcy or liquidation

In this case it will be useful to determine the point at which property in goods passes from the seller to the buyer

Specific Goods

Under the law, where there is a sale of specific goods the property in them will pass to the buyer at such time as the parties intend it to be transfer. And to ascer-tain that intention, there must be regard to the terms of the contract, the conduct of the parties and the circumstances of the case. Obviously if the parties specifi-cally agree on a particular event such as the payment of the price by the buyer or the delivery of the goods to the buyer, then the property will pass on the occur-rence of either event.

However, where there is no such agreement or their conduct does not indicate any other intention, property in the goods will pass in accordance the following rules: Where the contract of sale is unconditional and the goods are in a deliverable state, property in them will pass to the buyer at the time when the contract is made.

Where the seller is bound to do something to the goods to put them in deliverable state, property in them will not pass to the buyer until

127

that is done and the buyer is aware that it has been done. Thus in a sale of water pump affixed to the ground behind the Lusaka Pamodzi Hotel, property in the pump will not pass to the buyer until after it has been detached from its base and the buyer has been notified of that.

Where the goods are in a deliverable state but the seller has to do something to them to ascertain their price weigh, measure or test them) property in them will not pass until that is done and the buyer has noticed that it has been done.

Uncertained Goods

Property in this type of goods will not pass until after they have been ascertained, i.e. after they have been unconditionally appropriated to the contract by the seller with the buyer's assent or by the buyer with the seller's assent

Passing of Risk

Legally the position is that, in the absence of agreement to the contrary by the parties goods remain at the seller's risk until the property in them is transferred to the buyer and once property passes to the buyer, the goods are at his risk even though they may not have been delivered to him

The word 'risk' is used here in connection with accidental loss or destruction of the goods. As a result where goods are 'at the seller's risk' this means that if they are accidentally lost without fault on either side, being unable to deliver them to the buyer, the seller cannot recover their price already paid to him in advance. For the same reason, if they are at the buyer's risk and they get accidentally lost, he must pay the price even though he may not have taken possession of them as yet.

In other words, since the risk would be on the buyer, the loss would absolve the seller from his duty to deliver them and the buyer is obliged to accept delivery as if they conformed to the contract

Transfer of Title

Although the contract of sale of goods is about transfer of property in them to the buyer, it sometimes becomes necessary to deal with the issue of transfer of title. And that question often arises where a non – owner sells the goods and the issue is to determine who, as between their real owner and the buyer is entitled to them.

And the general rule is nemo dat quod non habet: the transfer of goods cannot pass a better title than that he himself has. Essentially this means that a buyer of goods from a thief does not get title to them since his seller does not have title in the first place. However, this rule is subject to the following exceptions whose effect is that a person with no title to goods or who has no authority to sell them can pass a good title in them to a third party.

Where the non-owner is an agent of the real owner of the goods and has actual or apparent authority from the latter to sell them. Where the real owner has by his conduct held out the non-owner as being the real owner of the goods. Where the goods are sold on the open market the buyer acquires a good title to them pro-vided he buys them in good faith. Where the seller has a voidable title (where he acquired the goods by misrepresentation, duress or under undue influence) but the title has not been avoided at the time of sale. Where the goods are sold without the owner's consent by a person exercising statutory power the buyer will get a good title for them. Implied Obligations in favour of the Buyer. The law imposes a number of obligations on the seller:

• Conditions
• Warranties

Where the buyer expressly or by implication discloses the purposes for which he requires the goods, it is an implied condition of the contract of sale that the goods will be reasonably suitable for that purpose.

Where there is a sale by sample, it is an implies condition of the contract of sale that the bulk will correspond with the sample in quality

Exclusion Clause

Of course with the exception of the implied condition relating to the seller's right to sell, all the other implied conditions can be excluded by an appropriately worded clause. The clause must be clear and unambiguous and must be part of the contract of sale of goods.

Performance of the Sale of Goods

In the performance of the contract of sale of goods, the seller and the buyer are under the following mutual obligations:

Delivery of the goods to the buyer

This is the seller's reciprocal duty to the buyer's obligations to accept the goods and pay for them

Generally 'delivery' can be defined as the voluntary transfer of possession of goods from the seller to the buyer

Of course the seller need not physically take the goods to the buyer; it suffices if he makes them available for the buyer to collect them or arrange for their collec-tion

In fact as shown below in the majority of cases the seller delivers goods to the buyer without physically transferring them at all

Delivery may be actual as where the seller transfers physical possession to the buyer or the buyer's agent

On the other hand delivery may be 'constructive' and not involve any physical transfer of goods at all

Construct delivery may take any one of the following forms:

Transfer of a document of title

- Delivery of an object giving physical control. The delivery to the buyer of keys to premises where the goods are stored is effective delivery of the goods to him
- Continuous possession. If the buyer was already in possession of the goods as bailee for the seller before making the contract of sale
- Delivery to a carrier: where in terms of the contract of sale the seller is authorised or required to send the goods to the buyer, their delivery to the carrier for transmission to the buyer is effective delivery to the buyer
- If the property has already passed to the buyer at the time of rejection, the action may be for damages or for the price of the goods

Payment for the Goods

The buyer is obliged to pay for the goods in accordance with the terms of the contract of sale Remedies for Breach of Contract Assuming that there has been breach of contract, the following remedies will be available to the parties.

Seller

If the property has passed to the buyer and he fails to pay for the goods, the seller can sue him for their price. If the seller is unpaid seller and he still has possession of the goods he can exercise the right of lien on them. The seller also has the right of stoppage of the goods. The unpaid seller also has right to resale the goods and recover from the proceeds of the unpaid price

The Buyer

For the buyer he has the following remedies: where the seller fails to comply with any one of the implied conditions, and the condition is not excluded the buyer can reject the goods and refuse to pay for them or recover the price he may have paid for them. As noted above where there is short or excessive delivery or the goods delivered are mixed with non – contract goods buyer is entitled to reject them.

Where the seller wrongfully neglects or refuses to deliver the goods, the buyer is entitled to sue him for breach of contract and recover as damages the estimated loss resulting from that breach. In the case of the seller's wrongful neglect or refusal to deliver the goods the buyer may also be entitled to specific perform-ance

Where the seller is in breach of warranty, or an implied condition but the buyer has accepted the goods so that the breach of condition can only be treated as a breach of warranty, the buyer is entitled to sue him for damages representing the loss resulting from that breach. It should be noted that in the absence of any agreement to the contrary where the buyer refuses to a accept goods delivered to him under circumstances where he is entitled to refuse delivery he is not bound to return them to the seller. It suffices to simply intimate to the seller that he refuses to accept them.

CHAPTER 19

Business Ethics

MANY BUSINESSES COMMENTATORS say that business ethics is critical and is a structured examination of how people and institutions should behave in the world of commerce. In particular, it involves examining appropriate constraints on the pursuit of self-interest, or (for firms) profits, when the actions of individuals or firms affect others. At the heart of business ethics is rightness or wrongness. For example is it morally right to engage in insider trading? Is it morally correct to be involved in corporate lies? However, many business commentators say that business ethics is the discipline of applying general ethical dilemmas in business dealings. According to Chris (2009) "BUSINESS ETHICS" is the study of ethical dilemmas, values, and decision-making in the world of commerce. It applies to all aspects of business conduct and is relevant to the conduct of individuals and business organizations as a whole.

Business ethics is a form of professional ethics that examines ethical principles

Applied eth-ics is a field of ethics that deals with ethical questions in many fields such as medical, technical, legal and business ethics.

Business ethics can be both a normative and a descriptive discipline. As a corpo-rate practice and a career specialization, the field is primarily normative. In aca-demia descriptive approaches are also taken. The range and quantity of business ethical issues reflects the degree to which business is perceived to be at odds with non-economic social values.

Business Ethics and the Changing Environment

Businesses and governments operate in changing technological, legal, economic, social and political environments with competing stakeholders and power claims. Stakeholders are individuals, companies, groups and nations that cause and re-spond to: external issues, opportunities and threats.

Internet and information technologies, globalization, deregulation, mergers and wars, have accelerated rate of change and uncertainty. In today's dynamic and complex environment stakeholders such as professionals, shareholders, manage-ment, employees, consumers, suppliers and members of community must make and manage business and moral decisions.

Environmental Forces and Stakeholders

Organizations are embedded in and interact with multiple changing local, na-tional and international environments. These environments are increasingly moving toward and emerging into a global system of dynamically interrelated interactions among local, national and international. A first step toward un-derstanding stakeholder issues is to gain an understanding of environmental forces that influence issues and stakes of different groups. This is a call to think globally before acting locally in many situations. As we discuss an overview of these environ-mental forces here, think of the effects and pressures each of the forces has on your industry, company, profession or career and job.

Stakeholder Management Approach

The question is: how do companies, communication media, political groups, con-sumers, employees, competitors and other groups respond when they are affected by an issue, dilemma, threat or opportunity from one or more of the environ-ments described? The stakeholder management approach is a way of understanding the effects of environmental forces and groups on specific issues that affect real – time stakeholders and their welfare.

The stakeholder approach begins to address these questions by enabling individu-als and groups to articulate collaborative, win – win strategies. The underlying aim here is to develop awareness of the ethics and social responsibility of different stakeholders' perceptions, plans, strategies and actions.

Business Ethics: Why Does It Matter?

Business ethicists ask, "What is right and wrong, good and bad, and harmful and beneficial regarding decisions and actions in and around organizational activities? Ethical "solutions" to business and organizational problems may seem available. Thus, learning to think, reason and act ethically can enable us to first be aware and recognize a potential problem.

"Doing the right thing" matters to all stakeholders. To companies and employers, acting legally and ethically means saving billions of dollars each year in lawsuits, settlements and theft. Studies have also shown that corporations also have paid significant financial penalties for acting unethically. Costs to businesses also in-clude: deterioration of relationships; damage to reputation; declining employee productivity; loyalty and absenteeism; companies that have a reputation of un-ethical and uncaring behaviour toward employees also have a difficult time re-cruiting and retaining valued professionals.

For business leaders and managers, managing ethically also means managing with integrity. Integrity cascades throughout an organization. It shapes and influ-ences the values, tone and culture of the organization, commitment and imagina-tion of everyone in a company. Then, we can evaluate our own and other's values, assumptions and judgments regarding the problem before we act. Laura Nash points out that business ethics deals with three basic areas of managerial decisions making. First, is a choice about what the laws should be and whether to follow them. Second, choices about economic and social issues out-side the domain of law, and lastly, choices about the priority of self – interest over the company's interest.

What Are Unethical Business Practices?

Surveys identify prominent everyday ethical issues facing businesses and their stakeholders. Recurring themes include: managers lying to employees or vice versa; office favouritism; taking credit for others' work; receiving or offering kickbacks; stealing from the company; firing an employee for whistle-blowing. padding expenses accounts to obtain reimbursements for quesionable business expenses; divulging confidential information or trade secrets commonly called insider trading; terminating employment without giving sufficient notice and using company property and materials for personal use.

9 Things That Ethics Promotes:

- Openness and transparency
- Honesty and integrity
- Excellence and quality
- Public accountability
- Legality
- Promote justice
- Confidential information
- Balanced decisions
- Whistle blowing

Relativism

Although relativism is most often associated with ethics, one can find defences of relativism in virtually any area of philos-ophy. Both relativism and morality in-volves the field of ethics, also called moral philosophy, which involves system-atic, defending and recommending concepts of right and wrong behaviour. The term ethics is also defined as a discipline involving inquiry into more judgments people make and the rules and principles upon which such judgments are based. There are two different versions of relativism: Factual Moral Relativism (FMR) and Normative Ethical Relativism (NER) as it is often claimed that moral beliefs are in fact relative.

It will be useful to generalize a distinction familiar from dis-cussions of ethical relativism and to distinguish FMR and NER with respect to anything that is claimed to be relative. Moral beliefs are in fact relative, that different people do make differ-ent moral judgments and advocates different more rules and princi-ples. Thus FMR claims about moral ideals and the like are often countered by arguments that such things are universal. Therefore FMR are empirical claims may tempt us to conclude that they are little philosophical interests, but there are sever-al reasons why this is so. This position is called FMR and as factual matter, the truth of FMR can be decided by empirical investigation. On the other hand, Normative Ethical Relativism (NER) is a claim that an

Act in Society S is right if and only if most people in society S believe A is right.

This is a Universal Normative Principal in so far as it applies to any person in society. However, the possibility of NER arises only when some action or practice is the locus of disagreement between holders of two self contained and exclusive systems. For example, two systems of beliefs, S1 and S2, are exclusive of one another when they have consequences that disagree un-der some description but do not require either to abandon their side of the disagreement. Thus a real confrontation between S1 and S2 would occur when S2 is real option for the group living under S1.

From the forgoing discussion we can conclude that NER seems to be a less pow-erful tool not robust enough and less convincing since in both society S1 and fails to understand why the same tool is interpreted differently. However, it is argued that if the principle of tolerance is accepted the society groups need not impose nor foster tolerance on moral beliefs on others.

On such NER can be accepted because it is the only norma-tive principal with commitment to tolerance. To their concepts, beliefs or modes of reasoning, then groups can not differ with respect to their concepts, beliefs or modes of reason-ing. Further, the NER supported by FMR takes on a more practical task, which is to arrive On one hand FMR does not necessarily deny the existence of a single correct moral appraisal, given the same set of circumstances. This means that FMR as a tool for supporting NER with empirical investigation NER in a given area tends to counsel tolerance of practices that conform to alterna-tives stan-dards prevailing in the area.

On the other hand FMR input into NER claims that different cultures have dif-ferent views of morality, which they unify under one general conception of mo-rality. FMR presupposes some measure of realism. For example if there are no such things as concepts, beliefs or modes of reasoning, then groups cannot differ with respect at more standards that regulate right and wrong conduct. Thus, this may involve articulating the good habit that we should acquire, the duties that we should follow in consequences of our behaviour on others.

Ethical Theory:
Cognitivism and Non-Cognitivism

The first and most profound division in ethical theory is between the claim that it is possible to know moral right from wrong and denial of that claim. Because this is claim and encounter-claim about what we can and cannot know, the position which declares we can know is called 'cognitivism' and the contrary position 'non cognitivism.' According to cognitivism there are objective moral truths which can be known, just as we can know other truths about the world. State-ments of moral belief, on this view can be true or false just as our statement that something is a certain colour can be true or false. According to the noncognitivist, by contrast, 'objective' assessment of moral belief is not possible.

It is all 'subjective'. There is no truth or falsity to be discovered. There is only belief, attitude, emotional reaction, and the like. As Hamlet puts it, 'There is nothing either good or bad but thinking makes it so'. When non-cognitivism claims that there are only attitudes, its proponents do not usually mean that moral judgments are simply expressions of one's feelings. Advocates of noncognitivism acknowledge the essentially social nature of morality by invariably arguing that these are group attitudes.

Consequentialism Versus Non- Consequentialism

The greatest divide in cognitivist thinking is between theories which assess moral right and wrong in terms of the consequences of actions and those which do not. Those which do are 'consequentialist' theories; those which do not are 'nonconse-quentialist'. With consequentialist theories we look to the re-sults of actions to determine the truth or falsity of moral judgements about them. If what follows from an action is, on balance, of benefit then it is, a good action and so we are right to do it. Conversely, if the outcome is, on balance harmful then the ac-tion is 'bad' and we are 'wrong' to do it.

For consequentialism the test of whether an action is right or wrong is whether it is good or bad in the sense of resulting in benefit or harm. In this case right or wrong is a question of good or bad; and good or bad a question of benefit or harm. For non-consequentialism, there is no immediate appeal to beneficial or harmful consequences to determine good or bad. A Divine Command theory offers an illustration of the difference between consequentialism and nonconsequentialism. If religious believers were to obey God's commands in order to attain a desirable state after death, or because they believed that obedience was rewarded by material success. Then such moves presuppose a consequentialist view of ethic. If, however, the believer obeys God's commands, not for any expected re-ward, but for the sole reason that God has commanded them, then he or she presupposes a strictly non-consequentialist account of morality. It is not what follows from our actions which then make them right or wrong but only the fact of their confor-mity or non-conformity to God's commands.

It is solely in virtue of being activities of such a conforming or non-conforming kind that actions are right or wrong and therefore good or bad. Taken item by item, a consequentialist and non-consequentialist listing of rights and wrongs will probably not differ very much. Of course there will be some disagreement on substantive moral issues and they are, unsurprisingly, likely to concern just those issues that divide society the most.

Utilitariasm: An Ethical of Welfare

The best known consequentialist theory of ethics is called 'utilitarianism'. The name derives from the use of the word utility to denote the capacity in actions to have good results. This choice of word proclaims the consequentialist nature of the the-ory. Utility means usefulness – under lying the point that it is the useful-ness of actions which determines their moral character than anything in the na-ture of the action itself.

Actions are not good or bad in themselves, but only in what they are good or bad for. Although, strictly speaking, good and bad are the results, while utility and disutility are the capacities for those results, they amount to the same thing in practice and can, for convenience, be treated as synonymous.

CHAPTER 20

Government Regulation

ALTHOUGH MOST ENTREPRENEURS RECOGNIZE the need for some government regulation of business, most believe the process is overwhelming and out of control. Government regulation of business is far from new. To date laws regulating business practices and government agencies to enforce the regulations have expanded continuously. Most entrepreneurs agree that some government regulation is necessary. There must be laws governing working safety, environmental protection, package labelling, consumer credit and other relevant issues because some dishonest, unscrupulous managers will abuse the opportunity to serve the public interest. It is not the regulations that protect workers and consumers and achieve social objectives that businesses object to, but those that produce only marginal benefits relative to their costs. Entrepreneurs especially seek relief from wasteful and meaningless government regulations, charging that the cost of compliance exceeds the benefits gained.

All businesses, regardless of type, must comply with statutes (laws passed by legislative bodies) and regulations (rules enacted by regulatory agencies to carry out the purposes of statutes). These statutes and regulations can come from all levels of government; federal, state, and local. Some of these statutes and regula-tions apply regardless of the nature of the business and, of course, a venture engaged in business in more than one state or local jurisdiction must comply with applicable laws and regulations from all applicable jurisdictions.

The enforcement agency has no obligation to notify the business that it must comply with the law. It is the business's obligation to inquire and comply. Fortu-nately, most agencies have public information departments eager to assist in providing information and obtaining compliance.

These laws and regulations include licensing and registration of business name, workers compensation, unemployment compensation, and permission to do business in a form other than a sole proprietorship. The collection of sales taxes and the withholding of employees' wages are further examples of obligations with which to comply.

The Occupational Safety and Health Administration (OSHA) has very specific requirements concerning health and safety which apply to many businesses' employees and customers. The enactment of the Americans with Disabilities Act (ADA) affects many businesses both in hiring practices and customer accommo-dations.

CHAPTER 21

Succession Planning

A BUSINESS THAT HAS BEEN ESTABLISHED DIES and to preserve the death we present what others have done to be successful. The question that comes to mind is what is a succession planning? Many writers in the field of en-trepreneurship say that succession planning is a process which deals with identi-fying and developing internal people with the potential to fill key busi-ness lead-ership positions in the company. This means that succession planning increases the availability of experienced and capable employees that are prepared to as-sume these roles as they become avail-able. Taken narrowly, "replacement plan-ning" for key roles is the heart of succession planning.

Succession Planning Process

The following steps should be followed: determine the key leaders for whom successors will be identified; identify the competencies of current key leaders; identify experience and duties required; identify personality, political savvy, judgement; iden-tify leadership skills; select the high-potential members who will participate in succession planning; identify gap between what the high-potential members are able to do presently and what they must do in the leadership role; create a development plan for each high-potential member to prepare him or her for the leadership position; perform development activities with each high-potential member; interview and select a member for the new leadership position and evaluate succession planning efforts and make changes to program based on evaluation for future programs.

Conclusion

THIS BOOK HAS EXAMINED entrepreneurship as a road to wealth creation at individual, firm (business) and state levels. In this book I have shown you how to step on the accelerator of wealth creation in an economy through entrepreneurship. This has been done by presenting to you a series of practical and proven methods that can work anywhere in the world. The departure from free market economy to mixed economy in which the individuals, firms (businesses) and the state are all players should be perceived as an engine of eco-nomic growth backed up by wealth creation. We are in an entrepreneurial and information age and the future of world economies will be greatly influenced by entrepreneurs with unique and innovative ideas. This book illustrates the evolu-tion of the entrepreneurship as well as characteristics of modern – day entrepre-neurs and state managers who practice transformation leadership. Entrepreneur-ship is an evolving process and would behove any individual interested in entering this process to take tour by completing this journey. This book is the first step.

REFERENCES

Books

Aaker, D.A. (2001), Strategic Market Managing, 6th ed. (New Jersey: John Wiley & Sons, Inc)

Aqualiano, N. (2001) Operations Management (New Jersey: McGraw – Hill Companies, Inc)

Bearden, L. (1990), 'Five Imperatives for improving service quality' (Great Brain: Ashford Colour Press)

Boyett, J. and Boyett, J. (1998), The Guru Guide (New Jersey: John Wiley & Sons, Inc)

Buswell, D. (1896), The development of quality measurement system for a UK

Blue's Clues for Success: The 8 Secrets Behind a Phenomenal Business by Diane Tracy (Dearborn, 2002).

Chandler, A. (1992) Strategy and Structure (Great Britain: MIT Press) Charan, R. and Tichy, N. (1999), Every Business is Growth Business: How your Company Can prosper year after year (New Jersey: John Wiley and Sons, Inc)

Chase, R. (2004), Competitive Edge (New Jersey: McGraw – Hill Companies, Inc) Church, G. (1999), Market Research: Methological Foundation, 7th ed. (London)

Cox, K. and Kotler P. (1998), Marketing Managing and Strategy: 4th ed. (New Jersey: Prentice Hall, Inc) Cohen, D, and Prusak, L. (2001), "How to Invest in Social Capital" Haward Business Review Volume 79 no. 6 pp 86 – 95 Cole, G.A. (1997) Management Theory and Practice, (Great Britain: Ashford Colour Press, Gosport) D, Aven R. (2002), "The Empire Strikes Back – Counter Revelatory Strategies for Industry Leaders" Harvard Business Review, Volume 80. no. 11, pp 69 – 79.

Daniels, J. (2004), International Business, (USA: Pearson Educational Limited)

David, F.R. (2001), Strategic Management – Concepts and Cases 8th ed. (New Jersey: Practice Hal, Inc) Doyley, P. (2002) Marketing Management and Strategy, 3rd ed. (USA: Pearson Education Limited) Duck, J. (1993:109), Managing Change: The Art of Balancing, Harvard Business Review August

East, R. (1997), Consumer Behaviour: Advances, and Application in Marketing (London: Prentice Hall, Inc)

Ellis, G. (2007), Zero to Million: How to Build a Company to One Million Dol-lars in Sales (New Jersey: McGraw – Hill Companies, Inc)

Gerson, R. (1994), Measuring Customers Satisfaction (London: Kegan Kegan Limited)

Guerrilla Marketing: Secrets for Making Big Profits from Your Small Business-by Jay Conrad Levinson (Mariner Books, 1998).

Harrigan, K. and Porter, M. (1983), "End – Game Strategies for Declining In-dustries" Harvard Business Review, July August.

Hisrich, R. (1998) Entrepreneurship, (USA: McGraw – Hill Companies, Inc)

Jeffrey, G. (2001:175), Journal of Business Venture, Harvard Business Review, July

Jones, G. (2005) How to launch and grow the new business, (Great Britain: Bell & Bain Ltd)

Karakaya, F., (2002), "Barriers to Entry in Industrial Markets" Journal of Busi-ness and Industrial Marketing, Vol. 17 Issue 5

Lash, L.M. (1920), "Care in service Business" Business and finance Review, pp26 – 30

Laura, M. (1996), Building Adaptive Firm, Small Business Forum (Great Brit-ain: Bell & Bain Lt)

McDonald, M. (1990), Marketing Plans: How to prepare them, How to use them, 4th ed (USA)

McConnell, C.R. and Brue, S.L. (2002). Economics (New Jersey: McGraw – Hill Companies, Inc)

McHugh, M. (2001), Understanding Business, (USA:McGraw – Hill Compa-nies, Inc)

Melkam, A. (1979), How to Handle Major Customers Profitably (USA: Butter - Heinemann)

Nellis, J. (2004), Essence of Business Economics (India: Prentice Hall Private Limited)

Nickles, W. McHugh, J. et al (2005), Understanding Business (New York: Mc-Graw – Hill Companies, Inc)

Oakland, J. (2001), Total Organizational Excellence – Achieving World – Class Performance (USA: Butterworth - Heinemann)

Olson, P. (1993), "Entrepreneurship Start – Up and growth" Business and Fi-nance Review, pp 5 – 20

Own Your Own Corporation: Why the Rich Own Their Own Companies and Everyone Else Works for Them by Garrett Sutton, Robert T.

Pardo, C. (1999), "Key Account Management in Business – to – Business Field: A French Overview" Journal of Business and Industrial Marketing, Vol. 14 Issue 4

Peters, M. (1998), Entrepreneurship, (USA:McGraw – Hill Companies Inc)

Porters, M. (1979), "How Competitive Forces Shape Strategy" Harvard Busi-ness Review March – April.

Portraits of Success: 9 Keys to Sustaining Value in Any Business by James Olan Hutcheson (Dearborn, 2002).

Potter, D. (1999), "Success Under Fire: Policies to Prosper in Hostile Time" California Management review, Winter, PP 24 – 38

Radebaugh, L. (2002), International Business, (USA: McGraw Hill Compa-nies, Inc)

Registrar of Companies Data Bank (2008)

Rigby, D. (2002), "Moving Upwards in Downturn" Harvard Business Review Vol. 80 no. 11,pp99-105 Robbins, S.P. (2001), Organizational Behaviour (New Jersey:Prentice Hall, Inc) Resnblun P. (2003), "Bottom Feeding for Blockbuster Business" Harvard Business Review Volume 81 no. 3, pp52 – 59

OECD (2012), "Regulatory framework: Starting a business", in OECD, Entre-preneurship at a Glance 2012, OECD Publishing. OECD (2011), "Tax incentives for business R&D", in OECD, OECD Science, Technology and Industry Scoreboard 2011, OECD Publishing.

OECD (2011), "Public support for business R&D", in OECD, Business Innovation Policies: Selected Country Comparisons, OECD Publishing. OECD (2010), Why Is Administrative Simplification So Complicated? Looking Beyond 2010, Cutting Red Tape, OECD Publishing.

OECD (2010), SMEs, Entrepreneurship and Innovation, OECD Studies on SMEs and Entrepreneurship, OECD Publishing. Saunders, M. Lewis P. et al (2000), Research Methods of Business Students, 2nd ed. (Great Britain: Ashford Colour Press Ltd)

Scarborough, M (2003), Effective Small Business, (USA: Pearson Education Limited) Schumpeter, J. (1996), An Intrinsic Desire to Succeed, (USA: Pearson Education Limited)

Spencer, R. (1999), "Key Accounts: Effectively Managing Strategic Complex-ity" Journal of Business and Industrial Marketing, Vol 14 Issue 4 Stalk, G. Stern, C (1998), "Perspective on Strategy from the Boston Consulting Group" (USA: John Wiley and Sons, Inc)

Stevenson, W. (2005), Operations Management, (New York: McGraw – Hill Companies, Inc)

Sullivan, D. (2001), International Business, (USA: Pearson Education Limited)

Wilson, D. (1999), Organizational Marketing (New Jersey: International Thosm-son Publishing)

World Bank (2013), Doing Business 2013: Smarter Regulations for Small and Medium-Size Enterprises, The World Bank Group, Washington, DC.

Young, E. (1993), "Entrepreneurship's Requisite Areas of Development: A Survey of Top Executives in Successful Entrepreneurial Firm" Journal of Business venture (March 1993)

Zimmer, T. (2000) An Entrepreneurial Approach, (USA: McGraw – Hill Compa-nies, Inc)

Magazines and Newspapers:

Black Enterprise <www.blackenterprise.com Business 2.0 <www.business2.com Business Startups <www.entrepreneur.com Business Week <www.businessweek.com Entrepreneur <www.entrepreneur.

com Fast Company www.fastcompany.com Forbes <www.forbes. com www.fortune.com

Franchise Handbook www.franchise1.com Harvard Business Review <www.harvardbusinessonline.com

Inc. www.inc.com Red Herring <www.redherring.com Wall Street Journal<www.wsj.com

Other Web Sites:

www.MrAllBiz.com business.lycos.com smallbusiness.yahoo.com www. aarpsmallbiz.com www.about.com/smallbusiness www.asbdc-us. org www.att.sbresources.com www.bcentral.com ww.bizland.com www.bloomberg.com www.business.gov www.busop1.com www. chamberbiz.com

www.entreworld.com www.isquare.com www.onlinewbc.gov www. quicken.com/small_business www.sba.gov www.score.org www. usatoday.com/money/smallbusiness/front.htm www.winwomen.org www.workz.com

Developing the Business Plan < http://www.fao.org/contact-us/terms/ en/>

Printed in the United States
By Bookmasters